Exclusive O

As our valued reader, your purchase of this book includes access to exclusive online resources designed to enhance your learning experience. These resources can be downloaded from our website, www.vibrantpublishers.com, and are created to help you apply Cybersecurity concepts effectively.

Online resources for this book include the following essential tools and templates:

1. **Important Cybersecurity Frameworks and Tools**
   - OWASP Top 10 Vulnerabilities
   - ISO/IEC 2001:2022
   - NIST Cybersecurity Framework
   - Top Threats to Cloud Computing 2024
   - CISA All Resources and Tools
   - ATT&CK Data and Tools
2. **Case Studies and Additional Resources**

Why these online resources are valuable:

- **Practical application:** The ready-to-use tools and frameworks will help you apply Cybersecurity processes in real-world scenarios.
- **Step-by-step guidance:** They enable a clear understanding of concepts, efficient implementation of techniques, and skill refinement.
- **Enhanced learning experience:** The case studies and additional resources will help reinforce knowledge and enhance your understanding of complex concepts.

How to access your online resources:

1. **Visit the website:** Go to www.vibrantpublishers.com
2. **Find your book:** Navigate to the book's product page via the "Shop" menu or by searching for the book title in the search bar.
3. **Request the resources:** Scroll down to the "Request Sample Book/Online Resource" section.
4. **Enter your details:** Enter your preferred email ID and select "Online Resource" as the resource type. Lastly, select "user type" and submit the request.
5. **Check your inbox:** The resources will be delivered directly to your email.

Alternatively, for quick access: simply scan the QR code below to go directly to the product page and request the online resources by filling in the required details.

bit.ly/slm-cs

Happy learning!

SELF-LEARNING MANAGEMENT SERIES

CYBERSECURITY ESSENTIALS
YOU ALWAYS WANTED TO KNOW

Setting the foundation for world-class cybersecurity practices

ELASTOS CHIMWANDA

CYBERSECURITY ESSENTIALS YOU ALWAYS WANTED TO KNOW

First Edition

Copyright © 2025, by Vibrant Publishers LLC, USA. All rights reserved. No part of this publication may be reproduced or distributed in any form or by any means, or stored in a database or retrieval system, without the prior permission of the publisher.

Published by Vibrant Publishers LLC, USA, www.vibrantpublishers.com

Paperback ISBN 13: 978-1-63651-488-8
Ebook ISBN 13: 978-1-63651-489-5
Hardback ISBN 13: 978-1-63651-490-1

Library of Congress Control Number: 2025935455

This publication is designed to provide accurate and authoritative information in regard to the subject matter covered. The Author has made every effort in the preparation of this book to ensure the accuracy of the information. However, information in this book is sold without warranty either expressed or implied. The Author or the Publisher will not be liable for any damages caused or alleged to be caused either directly or indirectly by this book.

All trademarks and registered trademarks mentioned in this publication are the property of their respective owners. These trademarks are used for editorial and educational purposes only, without intent to infringe upon any trademark rights. This publication is independent and has not been authorized, endorsed, or approved by any trademark owner.

Vibrant Publishers' books are available at special quantity discount for sales promotions, or for use in corporate training programs. For more information please write to bulkorders@vibrantpublishers.com

Please email feedback / corrections (technical, grammatical or spelling) to spellerrors@vibrantpublishers.com

Vibrant publishes in a variety of print and electronic formats and by print-on-demand. Some material included with standard print versions of this book may not be included in e-books or in print-on-demand. To access the complete catalogue of Vibrant Publishers, visit www.vibrantpublishers.com

SELF-LEARNING MANAGEMENT SERIES

TITLE	PAPERBACK* ISBN
BUSINESS AND ENTREPRENEURSHIP	
BUSINESS COMMUNICATION ESSENTIALS	9781636511634
BUSINESS ETHICS ESSENTIALS	9781636513324
BUSINESS LAW ESSENTIALS	9781636511702
BUSINESS PLAN ESSENTIALS	9781636511214
BUSINESS STRATEGY ESSENTIALS	9781949395778
ENTREPRENEURSHIP ESSENTIALS	9781636511603
INTERNATIONAL BUSINESS ESSENTIALS	9781636513294
PRINCIPLES OF MANAGEMENT ESSENTIALS	9781636511542
COMPUTER SCIENCE AND TECHNOLOGY	
BLOCKCHAIN ESSENTIALS	9781636513003
MACHINE LEARNING ESSENTIALS	9781636513775
PYTHON ESSENTIALS	9781636512938
DATA SCIENCE FOR BUSINESS	
BUSINESS INTELLIGENCE ESSENTIALS	9781636513362
DATA ANALYTICS ESSENTIALS	9781636511184
FINANCIAL LITERACY AND ECONOMICS	
COST ACCOUNTING & MANAGEMENT ESSENTIALS	9781636511030
FINANCIAL ACCOUNTING ESSENTIALS	9781636510972
FINANCIAL MANAGEMENT ESSENTIALS	9781636511009
MACROECONOMICS ESSENTIALS	9781636511818
MICROECONOMICS ESSENTIALS	9781636511153
PERSONAL FINANCE ESSENTIALS	9781636511849
PRINCIPLES OF ECONOMICS ESSENTIALS	9781636512334

*Also available in Hardback & Ebook formats

SELF-LEARNING MANAGEMENT SERIES

TITLE	PAPERBACK* ISBN
HR, DIVERSITY, AND ORGANIZATIONAL SUCCESS	
DIVERSITY, EQUITY, AND INCLUSION ESSENTIALS	9781636512976
DIVERSITY IN THE WORKPLACE ESSENTIALS	9781636511122
HR ANALYTICS ESSENTIALS	9781636510347
HUMAN RESOURCE MANAGEMENT ESSENTIALS	9781949395839
ORGANIZATIONAL BEHAVIOR ESSENTIALS	9781636512303
ORGANIZATIONAL DEVELOPMENT ESSENTIALS	9781636511481
LEADERSHIP AND PERSONAL DEVELOPMENT	
DECISION MAKING ESSENTIALS	9781636510026
INDIA'S ROAD TO TRANSFORMATION: WHY LEADERSHIP MATTERS	9781636512273
LEADERSHIP ESSENTIALS	9781636510316
TIME MANAGEMENT ESSENTIALS	9781636511665
MODERN MARKETING AND SALES	
CONSUMER BEHAVIOR ESSENTIALS	9781636513263
DIGITAL MARKETING ESSENTIALS	9781949395747
MARKETING MANAGEMENT ESSENTIALS	9781636511788
MARKET RESEARCH ESSENTIALS	9781636513744
SALES MANAGEMENT ESSENTIALS	9781636510743
SERVICES MARKETING ESSENTIALS	9781636511733
SOCIAL MEDIA MARKETING ESSENTIALS	9781636512181

*Also available in Hardback & Ebook formats

SELF-LEARNING MANAGEMENT SERIES

TITLE	PAPERBACK* ISBN
OPERATIONS MANAGEMENT	
AGILE ESSENTIALS	9781636510057
OPERATIONS & SUPPLY CHAIN MANAGEMENT ESSENTIALS	9781949395242
PROJECT MANAGEMENT ESSENTIALS	9781636510712
STAKEHOLDER ENGAGEMENT ESSENTIALS	9781636511511
CURRENT AFFAIRS	
DIGITAL SHOCK	9781636513805

*Also available in Hardback & Ebook formats

Table of Contents

1 Fundamentals of Cybersecurity — 1

1.1 Introduction to Cybersecurity   2
1.2 The CIA Triad   2
1.3 Importance of Cybersecurity   4
1.4 Cyber Threats, Vulnerabilities, and Attacks   7
1.5 Cybersecurity Awareness Training   19
Chapter Summary   20
Quiz   21
Case Study 1: Adoption of the CIA Triad   24

2 Cybersecurity Governance, Risk, and Compliance — 27

2.1 Cybersecurity Governance   28
2.2 Cybersecurity Risk Management   30
2.3 Cybersecurity Compliance   39
2.4 Cybersecurity Compliance Frameworks   40
Chapter Summary   45
Quiz   46

3 Physical Security — 51

3.1 Access Control   52
3.2 Physical Security Risks, Threats, and Vulnerabilities   57
3.3 Physical Security Controls   62
3.4 Physical Security Challenges   67
Chapter Summary   70
Quiz   71

4 Network Security — 75

4.1 Network Security Devices   76
4.2 Network Security Threats   82
4.3 Network Security Technologies   84

4.4 Wireless and Mobile Security   89
4.5 Network Monitoring   95
Chapter Summary   98
Quiz   99

5 Database Security   103

5.1 Types of Database Models   104
5.2 Components of a Database Management System (DBMS)   110
5.3 ACID Principles   112
5.4 Database Security Risks and Controls   114
5.5 Data Loss Prevention   118
Chapter Summary   123
Quiz   124

6 Cryptography   127

6.1 Introduction to Encryption   128
6.2 Encryption Methods   128
6.3 Encryption Mechanisms   130
6.4 Encryption Key Management   134
6.5 Hashing   139
6.6 Public Key Infrastructure (PKI)   144
Chapter Summary   148
Quiz   149
Case Study 2: Implementation of Encryption Strategies   153

7 Identity and Access Management   155

7.1 Introduction to IAM   156
7.2 Identification, Authentication, and Authorization   156
7.3 Identity Governance and Administration (IGA)   160
7.4 Identity as a Service (IDaaS)   165
7.5 Privileged Identity Management (PIM)   168
7.6 Emerging Technologies in IAM   171
Chapter Summary   175
Quiz   176

8 Security Testing — 181

   8.1 Vulnerability Assessments   182
   8.2 Penetration Tests   189
   8.3 Dynamic Testing   195
   8.4 Static Testing   197
   8.5 Secure Coding Practices   200
   Chapter Summary   203
   Quiz   204

9 Incident Management — 209

   9.1 Incident Response Process   210
   9.2 Tips for Improving an Incident Response   212
   9.3 Business Continuity and Disaster Recovery (BCDR)   214
   9.4 Disaster Recovery   217
   9.5 Cyber Forensics   221
   Chapter Summary   226
   Quiz   228

10 Cloud Security — 231

   10.1 Introduction to Cloud Security   232
   10.2 Cloud Service Models   233
   10.3 Cloud Deployment Models   236
   10.4 Importance of Cybersecurity in the Cloud   237
   10.5 The Shared Responsibility Model (SRM)   238
   10.6 Application Security   243
   10.7 DevSecOps   247
   Chapter Summary   252
   Quiz   253

Glossary — 279

Further Reading — 261

About the Author

Elastos Chimwanda has worked in the IT and cybersecurity field for over 15 years, gaining experience in various disciplines, such as vulnerability assessment, penetration testing, enterprise risk, cloud security, and regulatory compliance. As a thought leader and seasoned cybersecurity and cloud security expert, his goals include adding value, working efficiently and effectively, and sharing cybersecurity best practices to achieve overall success. Elastos started his career in IT auditing before moving on to concentrate on cybersecurity and cloud security. He holds a Bachelor of Commerce Honours Degree in Accounting and Information Systems and an MBA.

Elastos currently owns a cybersecurity practice dedicated to providing cutting-edge cybersecurity solutions. He is also a subject matter expert with esteemed professional bodies, including ISACA, ISC2, and CSA. Elastos holds numerous professional certifications, including CISSP, CCSP, CISA, and CCSK, and is an ISO/IEC 27001 Lead Auditor.

What Experts Say About This Book!

This book provides a well-structured and concise introduction to cybersecurity, allowing both beginners and professionals to build or reinforce their understanding. The layout is clean and easy to follow, with well-formatted tables, images, lists, case studies, and practice questions that enhance learning. It effectively covers a wide range of topics, from core concepts to cloud security and GRC, with strong coverage of database security, which is often underrepresented. Ideal for students, professionals, and certification candidates, this book can also support courses in IT fundamentals, security awareness, or introductory cybersecurity.

– **Jonathan Isley, Author,**
CompTIA CySA+ Certification Guide

Cybersecurity Essentials simplifies a complex field with clarity and purpose. Elastos Chimwanda has crafted a much-needed bridge between foundational cybersecurity knowledge and real-world application. An ideal starting point for students, business leaders, and professionals looking to break into the field.

– **Julio Bandeira de Melo, Cybersecurity Leader**

What Experts Say About This Book!

All good scholars always begin with the basics. In Cybersecurity Essentials, Elastos Chimwanda uses his long experience to build an introduction to cybersecurity. The book introduces and defines core terminology and explains where different terms might be encountered. The book covers terms from basic compliance and network security, through cryptography, testing, and incident management. If you are just starting your cybersecurity journey, this can point you in the right direction.

Each chapter has a great deal of definitional explanation, beginning with basic terms, discussing challenges, and then best practices. The book's latter half dives a little deeper into concepts such as cryptography, Identity and Access Management, and security testing. The author also dives into cloud security and the importance of sharing responsibility with a provider. One of the standout chapters was the Incident Response.

Overall, this book is a great start for anyone beginning their journey into cybersecurity. It introduces the right terms, the right thought patterns, and the correct questions to ask. Every term is carefully explained, and the chapters include follow-up questions to ensure the right message appears. If you are just starting your cybersecurity journey, this book can help ease your journey.

– Dr. Mark Peters, Retired USAF and Cybersecurity Author

Preface

Having started my career as an IT auditor, I have always been fascinated by the constant developments happening in IT. Throughout my professional career, I realized that in IT, you always need to keep pace with these developments to still be relevant, more so if you are in a position that provides advisory services to senior management and the boards. This is exactly what I adhered to.

Cybersecurity was not a topical issue until recently because the general populace was not exposed to technological developments like it is right now. Today, cybersecurity has become such a pressing issue that it is being talked about all over the world and on board agendas like never before. The increase in computer-based threats and attacks has further heightened the prominence of cybersecurity as a discipline. This is because professionals and business professionals are constantly trying to understand the causes and inner workings of cyber threats.

My experience in cybersecurity, both in leading teams and in consultancy, showed me that most organizations are still grappling with various challenges associated with cybersecurity. These include the shortage of qualified cybersecurity professionals, inadequate understanding of cybersecurity risks, and the inappropriate application of cybersecurity controls. Because of such challenges, the world is constantly seeing a proliferation of cyber-attacks, and huge losses are being incurred by both businesses and individuals.

I decided to embark on writing this book to raise awareness about the risks of cyber threats, aiming to reach readers with varying levels of knowledge. I realized that a foundational guide that explains the basics of cybersecurity could help people from all backgrounds—whether students or experienced professionals—to understand and better prepare for these risks.

As a seasoned professional in the cybersecurity field, having assisted a variety of organizations in successfully implementing cybersecurity standards and best practices, the least I could do is share my experiences. I am confident that you will find this book very useful in understanding the current dynamics involved in the cybersecurity industry. I envisage that by reading this book, you will have a grasp of cybersecurity issues that are very valuable in passing foundational exams or canting the needed foothold in the early stages of your career.

Introduction to the Book

In the current and ever-evolving technological space, many organizations have to grapple with the increased proliferation of cyber risks. This is so because advancements in technology also provide cyber threat actors with advanced tools and techniques to carry out even more sophisticated attacks. Organizations should, therefore, be able to keep pace with attackers to ensure maximum protection of technological assets. The major focus of the book is to enable you to understand the current methods and techniques used by cyber attackers, as well as how to counter these attacks when they do happen.

As cybersecurity professionals and the general public continue to adapt to constant advancements in technologies and attacker techniques, there may be some insufficiency and ineffectiveness if the processes are not handled appropriately. As we will see throughout this book, the way an organization handles its cybersecurity activities is wide-ranging, covering a broad spectrum of activities. For example, you will need to put in place effective IT governance structures, understand the processes of IT risk management, carry out penetration tests, perform cyber forensic investigations, and ensure business resilience in the event of incidents and disasters.

Of course, other factors are external to the organization that also need to be considered in any cybersecurity program. This includes compliance with laws, regulations, and standards and partnering with other organizations such as law enforcement agents. This strategically positions the organization to effectively carry out its cybersecurity programs and avoid costly penalties and fines in some cases.

Having said all this, there are certain expectations from reading this book. By the end of this book, you will be able to answer the following questions regarding concepts in the area of Cybersecurity:

- What is cybersecurity, and why is it important?
- What are the key functions within cybersecurity, and how do they interact with one another and the broader business?
- What are the key cyber threats that face organizations, and how can these threats be minimized?
- What are the general tools, techniques, and technologies that cybersecurity professionals and the general public can use to ensure they are always safe online?
- What are the responsibilities and decisions cybersecurity professionals think about?
- How will disruptions in the technological space impact the business world and our online security activities going forward?
- What are the practical applications of the knowledge gained around cybersecurity?
- What are the reasons for and the tools that are used to ensure the security of data in the cloud?

Who Can Benefit From This Book ?

- Students interested in understanding what a career in Cybersecurity may entail
- Cybersecurity analysts looking at how technological trends, threats, and disruptions may impact organizational operations
- Business professionals (especially non-technical) with limited exposure to cybersecurity or those who want a deeper understanding of cybersecurity operations
- Anyone with a desire to know more about the dynamic field of cybersecurity and its relevance in today's interconnected world

How to Use This Book?

I authored this book so that you could read it in just about any order you feel like, considering the assumed motivations of different readers. However, depending on your role, you may want to focus on appropriate sections of the book. For example:

1. If you›re just starting to learn about cybersecurity, start with Chapter 1 and read the book straight through to the end, making sure you understand new concepts along the way.
2. If you want to understand all the cybersecurity concepts for examination revision purposes, you should focus more on the multiple-choice questions found at the end of each chapter and go through the case studies provided in the book and in the online resources to brush up on your practical knowledge.
3. If you›re a member of the network security and penetration team, you need to check out the information in Chapter 3.
4. If you›re involved in database security, you may be interested to learn a variety of concepts discussed in Chapter 4.
5. If you know the basics of cybersecurity and you are transitioning to cloud security, Chapter 10 will provide you with helpful information.

Chapter 1
Fundamentals of Cybersecurity

Key Learning Objectives

- The definition and importance of cybersecurity
- Definitions and explanations for threats and vulnerabilities within the context of cybersecurity
- The CIA triad and its importance in cybersecurity
- Explanations for the most common forms of cyber attacks
- Mitigatory controls to address the risks of cyber attacks

This introductory chapter will provide an overview of cybersecurity and its importance, both for organizations and individuals. It defines cybersecurity and its importance, as well as the various types of threats and vulnerabilities found in organizations, and proposes mitigatory controls to reduce these to acceptable levels. The core purpose of this approach is to provide the reader with a strong understanding of the significant concepts commonly encountered in cybersecurity and prepare for further learning material.

1.1 Introduction to Cybersecurity

The current evolving digital dispensation has provided the global society with technological innovation. Organizations have spent decades increasing their online presence for various purposes, most importantly, to reach new customers. This increase in digital footprints has also led to a simultaneous escalation in cybercrime. The widespread use of the internet and growing access have made it easier for cybercriminals to target businesses and individuals, hence the need for cybersecurity. Cybersecurity applies technologies, processes, and control measures to protect the organization's information systems from unauthorized access, attacks, and damage.[1] It protects systems, networks, programs, devices, and data from cyber-attacks using technologies, processes, and controls. Ignoring cybersecurity, especially for small enterprises can lead to loss of reputation and infrastructure, reduced productivity and costly fines and/or penalties.

1.2 The CIA Triad

The CIA triad stands for confidentiality, integrity, and availability and is considered one of the most foundational concepts in cybersecurity. The term came into prominence due to cybersecurity professionals' realization that cybersecurity is not only about "confidentiality" but also about "integrity" and "availability". Satisfying these three elements and working in unison enhances any organization's overall cybersecurity. Figure 1.1 below shows the components that make up the CIA triad.

---

1. "Cyber Security." Accessed March 3, 2025. https://itgovernance.co.uk/what-is-cybersecurity

Figure 1.1 The CIA Triad

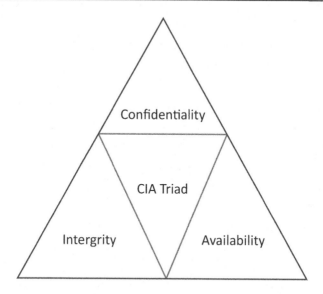

- **Confidentiality:** Confidentiality refers to the assurance that data and information are accessible only to authorized persons. This incorporates security measures such as data encryption, multi-factor authentication (MFA), and access controls that are implemented to prevent unauthorized access and data breaches. While preventing access to unauthorized users, the organization should also ensure that authorized users obtain access within properly defined privileges. For confidentiality to work effectively, organizational information should be classified and labeled.
- **Integrity:** Integrity is concerned with keeping the data accurate and unaltered during its various transfer and storage processes. Any unauthorized modification or tampering with data compromises its integrity, potentially leading to serious security risks. Integrity ensures that organizational data is trustworthy and can be relied upon by various stakeholders. Therefore,

measures to prevent tampering with data should be prioritized so that the data is preserved in its authentic state while in transit or at rest.

- **Availability:** Availability ensures that systems, data, and resources are accessible and usable by authorized individuals when required. It, therefore, involves protection against threats such as denial-of-service (DoS) attacks and system failures. DoS attacks overwhelm a system, thereby making it inaccessible to legitimate users. It is, therefore, critical to note that even if the information is kept confidential and integrity is maintained, it is only helpful if it can be provided to authorized users as and when required to perform various duties. This explains that availability is one of the critical components of the CIA triad, as it ensures that information is available for business use when requested by authorized personnel. This supports the smooth functioning of Information and Communication Technology (ICT) infrastructure, especially during disasters and other disruptions.

1.3 Importance of Cybersecurity

Overall, cybersecurity is crucial to any business because it maintains the integrity and reliability of an organization's information technology infrastructure and data and provides comfort over functions such as IT risk assessment, data integrity, IT security assessment, and disaster recovery. The following points explain why cybersecurity is important in the current digital age:

- **Provides security assurance:** Cybersecurity assists in identifying vulnerabilities in systems, preventing cyber-attacks, and protecting an organization's sensitive data over defined periods. Hence, it is essential to safeguard the organization's digital assets from attacks and ensure that the organization's IT systems are dependable and secure.

- **Ensures proper IT assets management:** Cybersecurity ensures that all the organization's IT assets are secure and have been properly deployed, managed, maintained, and updated. Through effective cybersecurity practices, organizations can protect their IT assets from unauthorized access, use, alteration, and destruction by identifying threats to those assets and taking steps to mitigate the identified risks.

- **Identifies and mitigates IT risks:** Cyber risks affect all assets in all IT areas of the organization. Through cybersecurity, the organization can identify and manage cyber risks. Cybersecurity professionals can recommend ways to mitigate cybersecurity risks by implementing security controls and being in line with the risk tolerance levels.

- **Ensures compliance:** Organizations are required to comply with cybersecurity laws and standards, including the Health Insurance Portability and Accountability Act (HIPPA), General Data Protection Regulation (GDPR), and Payment Card Industry Data Protection Standard (PCI DSS). We will be discussing these laws and regulations in the next chapter. Cybersecurity ensures the organization's adherence to such privacy and security regulations that are enacted from time to time. Through compliance, the organization maintains its reputation and is not affected by fines and other penalties that can arise from instances of non-compliance.

- **Ensures the integrity of data:** The integrity of organizational data is of utmost importance in conducting business operations. Cybersecurity helps to ensure that the organizational data and databases are accurate, updated, and dependable. The major objective is to assist the organization in effectively carrying out its responsibilities while also ensuring compliance with data protection regulations.

- **Ensures alignment of IT with business goals and objectives:** To be effective in the marketplace, the organization's IT initiatives and practices should align with the overall business objectives. Cybersecurity helps the organization to align its IT systems and practices with business objectives, thereby supporting the achievement of the organization's strategic goals and objectives. Fewer incidences and impacts from cyber attacks allow an organization to concentrate on its core business.

- **Improves efficiency:** Overall, undertaking cybersecurity enables an organization to discover inefficiencies in its IT processes that may indicate compromise and attacks. This detection allows the organization to address such deficiencies ere they become risks to the achievement of objectives. Through proper cybersecurity practices, an organization can pinpoint the exact IT products and services required for maintaining and enhancing security.

- **Protects information assets:** Cybersecurity is a fast-evolving field that continually poses new challenges for companies, government agencies, and individuals. Since data breaches and cyberattacks are more common than ever, cybersecurity involves protecting computers from viruses and other types of malware using antivirus software or other security programs. It also includes safeguarding information assets to prevent data theft, which could lead to liability risks for the organization. Additionally, devices need protection, and network connections and data backups must be secured at all times.

1.4 Cyber Threats, Vulnerabilities, and Attacks

The concepts of threats, attacks, and vulnerabilities are crucial to the foundational understanding of cybersecurity. The following provides a brief description of these concepts.

1.4.1 Cyber Threats

Regardless of its size, the entire digital landscape of an organization represents a potential entry point for cyberattacks. These can include social media accounts, mobile devices, technological infrastructure, people, and cloud services. These are known collectively as the "threat landscape". Notice that the threat landscape can cover more than just computers and mobile phones. It can include any elements owned or managed by an organization or some that are not. Organizations should invest in Cyber Threat Intelligence (CTI) and leverage tools such as the STRIDE Threat Model[2] to ensure they are well-versed regarding the common cyber threats at any given time.

1.4.2 Cyber Vulnerabilities

A vulnerability is any weakness or flaw in the organization and its systems that attackers can exploit. When a threat exploits a vulnerability, the risk of attack increases. It is crucial for organizations to be up to date with common vulnerabilities at any given time. You can achieve this by accessing various vulnerability databases such as the

---

2. STRIDE is a threat modeling methodology developed by Microsoft to identify and categorize potential security risks in software applications, focusing on six key threat types: Spoofing, Tampering, Repudiation, Information Disclosure, Denial of Service, and Elevation of Privilege. See https://www.microsoft.com/en-us/security/blog/2007/09/11/stride-chart/ for more information

Common Vulnerabilities and Exposures (CVE).[3] The most common vulnerabilities are due to system misconfiguration and include the following:

- Not removing errors from applications
- Having settings that leak information
- Running outdated software
- Running unnecessary services, thereby increasing the attack surface
- Not changing default keys and passwords
- Not training users

1.4.3 Cyber Attacks

A cyber attack is an attempt to gain illegal access to organizational systems to cause damage or harm. It typically results in someone gaining unauthorized access to devices, services, or networks (security breach) and performing undesirable actions on the organization's IT resources. The impact of a cyber-attack can range from minor impacts, such as an inconvenience for an individual in accessing authorized resources, to global economic and social disruptions costing millions of dollars in terms of damage. Some of these undesirable actions include the attacker doing the following:

- Encrypting files and demanding a ransom
- Removing vital information to cause serious harm
- Infecting systems with malware
- Stealing information
- Stealing credentials (credential theft)

---

3. The Common Vulnerabilities and Exposures system provides a reference method for publicly known information-security vulnerabilities and exposures. Visit https://www.cve.org/ for more information.

- Publicly exposing private information without authority
- Interfering with the proper functioning of critical business processes and systems

An "attack vector" is an entry point or route an attacker uses to gain access to a system. The following are some of the common attack vectors:

- **Email:** This is perhaps the most common attack vector. Cybercriminals send seemingly legitimate emails that result in users acting unaware. The actions a user is often tricked into performing include downloading a file or selecting a link that will compromise their device.
- **Removable media:** An attacker can use media such as USB drives to compromise organizational systems. For instance, an attacker may copy and load malicious code into USB devices that are subsequently provided to users, and when these are plugged into organizational systems, they spread malware throughout the organization.
- **Downloads:** Attackers can lure you into downloading malicious software on their devices or systems. When the devices get compromised, they provide an entry point into the organization's wider system or network.
- **Cloud services:** As more organizations rely on cloud services, this is also becoming an attack vector as attackers compromise poorly secured resources or services in the cloud. For example, an attacker could compromise an account in a cloud service to gain control of any resources or services accessible to that account's associated resources.
- **Insiders:** Insiders in the form of employees can serve as an attack vector in a cyberattack, whether intentionally or not. For example, you might become the victim of

a cybercriminal who carries out a social engineering attack through impersonation and, therefore, gains unauthorized access to a system. In this instance, you serve as an unintentional attack vector; however, in other cases, an employee with authorized access may use it to steal or cause harm to an organization intentionally.

Table 1.1 below explains some common cyber-attacks that companies frequently have to protect themselves against.

Table 1.1 Common Cyber Attacks

Type of Attack	Description
DoS and DDoS	A denial of service (DoS) is an attack designed to overwhelm an organization's resources to the point that it becomes unable to respond to legitimate business requests, which delays time-critical operations in the organization.[4] Therefore, the DoS is a typical example of an attack on availability. A distributed denial-of-service (DDoS) attack drains all the resources of a system, often resulting in a complete system shutdown.
Social engineering attacks	Attackers use tricky methods to exploit or manipulate users into performing actions that grant the attacker unauthorized access to a system. There are various forms of social engineering attacks, including the following: • **Impersonation:** An impersonation attack happens when an attacker gains the trust of an authorized user by posing as an authorized person to access a system for some nefarious activity. For example, an attacker may pose as a maintenance engineer and trick users into revealing their passwords. The attacker then used the passwords to access an organization's systems without authority.

---

4. "Understanding Denial-of-Service Attacks | CISA," February 1, 2021.
https://www.cisa.gov/news-events/news/understanding-denial-service-attacks.

Type of Attack	Description
	• **Phishing:** A phishing attack is perpetrated when an attacker fools a user into performing some act detrimental to the security, such as opening attachments infected with malware. Phishing has many variants, such as whaling (targeting high-level executives) and spear phishing (targeting a certain category of employees), and these constitute some of the major forms of social engineering attacks. The major challenge with phishing is that its targets are often unaware they are under attack, which allows the attacker to move laterally across the organization's systems.
Malware	Malware, also known as malicious software, refers to unwanted software installed on the organization's system without authorization. Such an installation aims to infect other systems in the organization through legitimate websites, web applications, and attachments. Attackers can also use malware to steal data and disclose confidential information about an organization. There are several types of malware, including the following:
	• **Virus:** A virus is a form of malware that can infect all the files on an organization's networks. It is considered one of the most challenging types of malware to mitigate as it can replicate itself by inserting its malicious code into other programs across the entire organization.
	• **Worm:** A worm can infect the entire network quickly as it requires no end-user involvement in its replication; it can self-replicate, thereby affecting many systems in a short period.

Type of Attack	Description
	• **Trojan:** Trojans are also considered one of the most challenging forms of malware to detect due to their ability to disguise themselves as legitimate and often innocent programs. However, as soon as the victim executes the malicious code and instructions, a Trojan can function independently, affecting organizational systems frequently without the user's knowledge. Attackers usually deploy Trojans to provide an entry point for other forms of malware. • **Adware:** Adware is a form of malware in which end-users are served unwanted and unsolicited advertising, such as contact pop-ups that appear on opening web pages. • **Spyware:** This type of malware is installed by attackers to collect sensitive data such as user IDs and passwords without the end-user suspecting anything. This sensitive data can then be used to gain unauthorized access to organizational systems. • **Ransomware:** Ransomware is generally known as one of the most dangerous malware attacks that can affect an organization. It works by infecting the organization's system, encrypting files, and holding onto the encryption key until the victim pays a ransom. This ransom is mainly in the form of cryptocurrency. This has led to many organizations losing huge sums of money to cybercriminals. Oftentimes, attackers write ransomware code and sell it to hackers who then launch attacks, a phenomenon known as Ransomware-as-a-Service (RaaS).

Type of Attack	Description
Password attacks	Passwords are one of the most common authentication tools used to provide access to authorized individuals to organizational systems. However, they are often a weak form of authentication and vulnerable to several types of attacks, including brute-force attack methods and dictionary attacks. In a brute force attack, the attacker tries several random multiple combinations of letters, words, and symbols that may be used in creating passwords.[5] In contrast, in a dictionary attack, the attacker uses a preset list of words (called a dictionary) to crack passwords.
Web attacks	A web attack is any attack that targets the web, including web applications. Any organization carrying out business online is at risk from web attacks. Common web attacks include: • **SQL injection**—An SQL injection is an attack that exploits weaknesses in databases. It employs an SQL query sent from the client to a database on the server to inject a harmful, malicious command. As the server is unaware of the injections, it runs the command, thereby allowing the attacker to penetrate organizational systems. • **Cross-Site Request Forgery (CSRF):** A CSRF attack involves a user conducting some action online that benefits the attacker. The major objective of a CSRF attack is to steal credentials from the victim, which are then used for subsequent criminal activities. For example, the victim may click on a link that runs a script that changes login credentials. This allows the attacker to access web applications by logging in as a legitimate user. Figure 1.2 below illustrates a CSRF attack in action.

---

[5]. Ayers, Rick, Sam Brothers, and Wayne Jansen. "Guidelines on Mobile Device Forensics." National Institute of Standards and Technology, May 2014. https://doi.org/10.6028/NIST.SP.800-101r1.

Figure 1.2 CSRF Attack

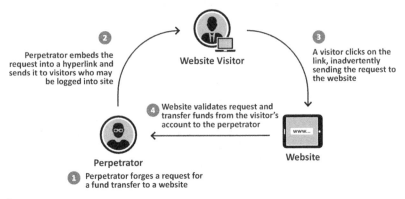

Source: https://www.imperva.com

Type of Attack	Description
Business Email Compromise (BEC)	A business email compromise (BEC) attack involves an attacker targeting specific individuals, usually employees who authorize payments. The attackers seek to deceive such personnel into transferring funds into the accounts owned by themselves or accounts they control or divulging confidential information through the manipulation of email processes.[6] This has resulted in huge financial losses for the targeted organizations.
Insider threats	Humans are the weakest link in the cybersecurity continuum, and because of that, they constitute one of the dangerous loopholes for attackers. Insider threats are difficult to control because insiders are aware of the organization's security weaknesses and are, therefore, better placed to evade existing controls. Insiders have legitimate access to organizational systems and infrastructure, some with privileged access. This makes the likelihood of insiders conducting successful attacks higher than that of external attackers.

---

6. *What Is Business Email Compromise (BEC)? | Microsoft Security.* https://www.microsoft.com/en-us/security/business/security-101/what-is-business-email-compromise-bec. Accessed 15 Sep. 2024.

Type of Attack	Description
Adversary-in-the Middle Attack (MiMA)	A adversary-in-the-middle attack (MiMA) involves an attacker positioning themselves in the middle of communication flow to intercept data and information flowing through the channel. The objective is to steal or alter the data somehow and is employed for spying purposes and providing intelligence for a more sophisticated attack later. The cybersecurity professional should note that the presence of AiMA, even in its immaterial form, constitutes an elevated threat to the organization as the attacker can gain additional systems privileges to conduct more damaging attacks.
MFA fatigue	MFA fatigue is a form of attack that involves the attacker flooding the system with multiple requests for MFA authentication with the expectation that out of fatigue, the user will eventually accept the requests. Hence it was also known as MFA flooding or MFA bombing. This type of attacks shows that users should always be diligent even in environments where MFA is in place.
Supply chain breaches	These attacks happen as a result of vulnerabilities on the supply-side. If your suppliers have weaknesses in their systems and networks, cyber attackers can exploit these to inflict harm on your environment. For example, a supplier may not be patching their systems providing an entry point for attackers, thus affecting all organizations within that supply chain.
Emerging attacks	The rise in the use of emerging technologies such as Artificial Generative Intelligence (AI), Web3, and blockchain has led to emerging attacks. Common forms of attacks include the use of AI to generate deep fakes, phishing content, and malicious code. Attackers are also taking advantage of smart contract vulnerabilities to undertake criminal activities such as crypto wallet thefts.

1.4.4 Mitigating Cyber Attacks

An organization should have a mitigation strategy to deal with various cyber-attacks. Such strategies are sometimes referred to as countermeasures. A mitigation strategy relates to an organization's steps to prevent or defend against a cyberattack and usually entails the implementation of technological and organizational policies and processes designed to protect against attacks. The following are some of the many different mitigation strategies available to an organization:

- **Attack Surface Management (ASM):** This refers to the practice of minimizing entry points for attackers within your environment. Examples include reducing assets that are subject to exposure, disabling unnecessary accounts and continuously monitoring the environment. This allows you to discover and monitor their external-facing digital assets and apply the necessary controls in a timely manner.

- **Multi-Factor Authentication (MFA):** Traditionally, if someone's password or username is compromised, this allows a cybercriminal to gain control of the account. In light of this, MFA was introduced to combat this and works by requiring a user to provide multiple forms of authentication for verification purposes. These factors range from something the user knows (knowledge factor), such as a Personal Identification Number (PIN), something the user has (biometric factor), such as a fingerprint, or something the user possesses (possession factor), such as a phone.

- **Zero trust principle:** In today's global economy, powered by cloud technologies, data is everywhere and accessed from anywhere. The zero trust security principle is an information security principle that states no one should be trusted to access an organization's systems. Figure 1.3 depicts the main concepts of zero trust.

Figure 1.3　The Zero Trust Principle

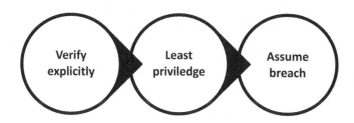

As shown in Figure 1.3 above, the principle calls for thorough verification through identification and authentication methods and assuming breach before granting access.

- **Implement people controls:** The organization should always perform thorough verification and background checks, especially on all organizations and third parties. Cybercriminals tend to hide through legitimate interests, as suppliers when they have other motives. Background checks and other forms of people controls assist the organization in weeding out cybercriminals for genuine business associates.
- **Virtual Private Network (VPN):** A VPN allows you to maintain your privacy while navigating the internet. It makes online activities virtually untraceable by masking the Internet Protocol (IP) address and should be deployed to enhance security. VPNs can also be used to establish secure and highly encrypted connections.
- **Firewall:** A firewall monitors and filters incoming and outgoing network traffic by the organization's defined

security policies. It works by segmenting a private internal network and the Internet at its primary level. It blocks virtual harmful traffic while allowing secure and non-threatening traffic to flow uninterrupted through the network. There are many types of firewalls, and they come as both hardware and software. The organization should ensure that it obtains the appropriate firewall per its requirements and that it is appropriately placed in the organization's network.

- **Encryption:** Encryption employs an algorithm to convert plain text into cipher text to protect data and information whether in transit, in process, or at rest. This process renders the message useless unless it has been decrypted. Decryption is a process of converting the ciphertext back into its plain text form so that it can be understood. Data encryption and decryption are made possible by using encryption keys. Encryption is discussed in more detail in Chapter Four of this book.

- **Perform regular software updates:** One of the significant causes of cyber-attacks has been unpatched software, which provides an easy entry point for attackers. Updating the software regularly provides the organization with the necessary updated features, bug fixes, and security updates, which enhances security. The organization should always ensure its software is updated to the latest version.

- **Perform regular vulnerability assessments and penetration tests:** Vulnerability assessments and penetration tests (popularly known as VAPTs) allow the organization to identify any vulnerabilities that may be available in its systems and networks. Vulnerability assessments scan for vulnerabilities and exploit them to identify vulnerabilities and determine the extent to which attackers can inflict harm on the organization's IT infrastructure.

- **Backup critical data:** While the organization can take all measures to prevent attacks, some attacks happen regardless of the controls in place. This results in the loss of sensitive information and security breaches, affecting organizational business continuity. By backing up data, the organization can quickly restore that data and continue operations in case of a successful attack and eventual data loss. It is also crucial to ensure the data is stored securely, preferably off-site.

1.5 Cybersecurity Awareness Training

Every organization is secure once its people understand and are knowledgeable about security risks and are educated enough to recognize signs of security attacks and how to respond to them. The adage that humans are the weakest link in the security chain still holds in contemporary cybersecurity studies. Therefore, the organization should educate its employees on all aspects of information security. Organizations can defend against cybersecurity attacks by educating their staff regarding how to:

- Identify and recognize suspicious message elements.
- Understand actions to take when they spot anything suspicious
- Avoid responding to external requests for personal information
- Lock devices when they are not in use
- Strictly follow organizational policies when storing, sharing, or destroying data.

Chapter Summary

- Cybersecurity is a crucial aspect of society as it involves assessing an organization's security threats and implementing measures to reduce them.

- Cybersecurity encompasses the entire organization and its infrastructure, including its systems and networks.

- The CIA triad is an essential term in cybersecurity, emphasizing the interplay of confidentiality, integrity, and availability.

- A cybersecurity attack is any attempt to gain unauthorized access to systems to cause harm or damage. These attacks take many forms, including phishing, DoS, malware, and password attacks, among others.

- Vulnerabilities represent flaws or weaknesses in the organization's security posture that attackers can exploit. These include human error and running outdated systems.

- Organizations must understand the role of cybersecurity in implementing the overall cybersecurity architecture and selecting countermeasures.

Quiz

1. Cybersecurity has led to various forms of digital disruptions worldwide. Which of the following are the results of this trend?
   a. Enhanced physical security
   b. Rapid technological innovation
   c. Decreased online presence globally
   d. Reduced cybercrimes

2. A lot of organizations have increased their online presence. What is the motivation behind this?
   a. To reduce operating costs
   b. To reach new market segments
   c. To reduce cybercrime
   d. To cut their digital footprints

3. Why is cybersecurity considered an essential requirement by most business organizations?
   a. To enhance physical security
   b. To protect against disasters
   c. To prevent unauthorized cyber-attacks
   d. To increase cybercrime

4. What does the acronym CIA stand for in the field of cybersecurity?
   a. Confidentiality, Integrity, Availability
   b. Confidentiality, Information, Authentication
   c. Confidentiality, Integrity, Authentication
   d. Confidentiality, Information, Access

5. Which of the following is a common control used to enhance confidentiality?
   a. Encryption
   b. Software updates
   c. CCTV
   d. Disaster recovery plan

6. Cybersecurity is crucial for business operations because:
   a. It increases business resilience
   b. It maintains the confidentiality, integrity, and availability of IT infrastructure and data
   c. It reduces the need for skilled IT staff
   d. It reduces the extent of cybercrime

7. Cybersecurity is often associated with IT risk management. What is the critical relationship between cybersecurity and IT risk assessment?
   a. Reduces the need for IT risk assessment
   b. Leads to an increase in overall software and hardware costs
   c. Eliminates the need for performing software updates
   d. Enhances the overall security posture of the organization, thereby reducing cyber risks

8. How does cybersecurity ensure proper IT asset management?
   a. It reduces the number of IT assets required
   b. It ensures that IT assets are securely managed
   c. It increases the number of IT assets required in the organization
   d. It supports the outsourcing of IT assets

9. What is one of the crucial roles cybersecurity professionals play in managing cyber risks?
   a. Increasing internet access
   b. Recommending to executive management ways to mitigate cybersecurity risks
   c. Advocating for the reduction in the number of employees
   d. Promoting the enhancement of physical security controls

10. CD Pharmaceutical is a firm operating in the drug business in Europe and allows payments through credit cards. Which of the following regulations must CD comply with?
    a. Health Insurance Portability and Accountability Act (HIPPA)
    b. General Data Protection Regulation (GDPR)
    c. Payment Card Industry Data Protection Standard (PCI DSS)
    d. All of the above

Answers

1 – b	2 – b	3 – c	4 – a	5 – a
6 – b	7 – d	8 – b	9 – b	10 – d

Case Study 1

Adoption of the CIdA Triad

Overview

CDC Ltd. is a hypothetical consultancy firm that provides a variety of cybersecurity services, including penetration testing and vulnerability assessments in Johannesburg. It has a modest staff complement of employees, a total of 20 professionals who are skilled in their various specialties. The firm serves a wide range of clients in a variety of industries, spanning from governance departments to finance, healthcare, and retail. One of the major aspects that CDC Ltd. takes seriously is cybersecurity, as it handles clients' sensitive information.

Provisions of the CIA Triad

CDC Ltd. abides by the strict provisions of cybersecurity as stipulated in the CIA triad as follows:

- **Confidentiality:** CDC Ltd implemented strict access controls, data encryption, and Multi-Factor Authentication (MFA) to ensure that only authorized personnel could access sensitive data. The firm has categorized and tagged organizational information so that it can be dealt with correctly. Periodic security awareness training was performed to inform people of data protection practices.

- **Integrity:** To maintain data integrity, CDC Ltd. adopted measures to prevent unauthorized modifications. In the process, they incorporated digital signatures and checksums to ensure data integrity while in transmission and storage. Furthermore, strong backup and recovery procedures were put in place to restore data in the event of either accidental or intentional modifications.

- **Availability:** When deploying systems and data, CDC Ltd. took measures to meet demands by providing redundancies in infrastructure and providing regular system service. The firm has also recently implemented Distributed Denial-of-Service (DDoS) protection technology. The reason behind this was to reduce incidences of DDoS attacks. To enhance availability, the forms also crafted and implemented a disaster recovery plan (DRP). This plan was designed to enable the firm to effectively prepare for andd recover from disasters.

Impact

The Managing Parent (a hypothetical organization) has confirmed that by effectively adopting the CIA Triad, CDC Ltd. was able to enhance its cybersecurity significantly. The firm managed to reduce the risk of cyber-attacks from 50% to 5% within the past year. The firm also witnessed fewer incidents of unauthorized access, data breaches, and system downtime. This has resulted in increased client confidence and satisfaction, which in turn helped to improve the trustworthiness and market standing of CDC Ltd.

Discussion Questions

1. How did CDC Ltd. take measures to protect data privacy, and why are these measures significant?
2. Explain how the firm was able to maintain data integrity. What are the potential risks of not addressing data integrity?
3. What strategies did CDC Ltd. use to ensure system availability, and how did these strategies benefit the company during unexpected events?

Chapter 2
Cybersecurity Governance, Risk, and Compliance

Key Learning Objectives
- The definitions and importance of cybersecurity governance, risk, and compliance
- Definitions and explanations for risk management within the context of cybersecurity risk
- Explanations for the most common forms of cybersecurity compliance frameworks
- The controls that can be deployed to mitigate the risks of cyberattacks

Cybersecurity professionals should understand the implementation and functioning of cybersecurity governance, risk, and compliance (GRC) processes as they influence the organization's cybersecurity strategies and activities. This chapter will discuss the principles of cybersecurity GRC and their respective roles.

2.1 Cybersecurity Governance

Cybersecurity governance refers to how an organization controls and directs its approach to cybersecurity. It consists of processes that ensure that cybersecurity activities support and enable the achievement of an organization's objectives. It involves defining responsibilities and decision-making processes, establishing policies and procedures, and implementing controls to ensure cybersecurity resources are used effectively and efficiently.

2.1.1 Role of Cybersecurity Governance

Effective cybersecurity governance is crucial for an organization's objectives as it enables it to manage its risks, align cybersecurity strategies with business objectives, and ensure the value delivery of cybersecurity investments. The following are some benefits of cybersecurity governance.

- **Accountability:** Cybersecurity governance provides transparency, accountability, and assurance in the way resources are used by legal and regulatory requirements to achieve cybersecurity objectives. Therefore, it plays a key role in supporting and enabling business success.

- **Alignment of cybersecurity investments:** Implementing cybersecurity governance structures ensures that the organization's cybersecurity investments are aligned with business strategies and goals, enabling organizations to make informed decisions about project prioritization and resource allocation.

- **Assists in risk management:** Cybersecurity governance helps organizations manage cyber risks by identifying and addressing vulnerabilities, ensuring data protection, and complying with legal and regulatory requirements.

- **Drives innovation:** Cybersecurity governance is a technical function and a strategic enabler for organizations. By aligning cybersecurity strategies with business objectives, organizations can leverage technology to gain a competitive advantage, improve operational efficiency, and drive innovation. For example, cybersecurity governance can inspire an organization to devise new ways and solutions to address cyber threats.
- **Assists in performance management:** Cybersecurity governance provides a framework for organizations to evaluate and measure the performance of their cybersecurity investments. It helps in the establishment of metrics, such as key performance indicators (KPIs), that can be applied in performance management.
- **Promotes a compliance culture:** By implementing cybersecurity governance, the organization brings a culture of order in managing cybersecurity processes, thus simplifying compliance with legal, regulatory, and other requirements.

2.1.2 Challenges of Cybersecurity Governance

Cybersecurity governance has challenges that must be addressed to enhance its effectiveness. The following are some significant challenges associated with an audit of cybersecurity governance.

- **Resistance to change:** Employees and management usually need to be more comfortable with the adoption of recent emerging concepts such as cybersecurity because they fear the unknown. They may, therefore, refuse to cooperate or try to sabotage cybersecurity governance initiatives. The organization should employ specialized human relations skills to allay these fears by emphasizing the benefits of conducting governance audits.

- **Resource constraints:** Resource constraints may also hinder the success of cybersecurity governance initiatives in organizations with limited budgets. Vast amounts of resources are often required to undertake cybersecurity governance projects successfully. Therefore, organizations should ensure adequate resources are allocated before commencing any cybersecurity projects.
- **The complexity of cybersecurity governance risks and controls.** The dynamic nature of the elements comprising the whole discipline of cybersecurity governance, such as cybersecurity risk assessment, adds to the complexities of implementing cybersecurity governance activities in most organizations.

2.2 Cybersecurity Risk Management

Cybersecurity risk management identifies, prioritizes, and manages cyber risks in an organization.[7] It also involves designing procedures to minimize the impact of such risks on the organization's resources. You should note that cyber risk cannot be eliminated; it can only be mitigated, avoided, transferred, or accepted.

Adopting cyber risk management aims to reduce cyber risk to an acceptable level under the organization's risk tolerance and appetite. Cybersecurity risk management is very critical to the success of cybersecurity governance

---

7. "What Is Cyber Risk Management? | IBM," May 25, 2023. https://www.ibm.com

as a discipline due to the prevalence of risks that often characterize cybersecurity environments.

In light of this, a brief background on risk management is crucial for cybersecurity security professionals. The following definitions are critical for any discussion involving cybersecurity risk management.

2.2.1 Cyber Risk Concepts

- **Risk:** ISC2 defines risk as the possibility of damage and the likelihood that damage will be realized.[8] Therefore, anything that affects, hinders, or obstructs the organization from its objective can be viewed as a cybersecurity risk. The relationship between a threat and a vulnerability giving rise to risk is depicted in Figure 2.1.

Figure 2.1   Risk

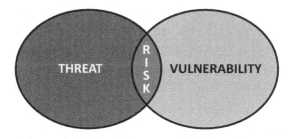

Source: : https://www.infosectrain.com

---

8. "CISSP Glossary - Student Guide." Accessed March 29, 2025. https://www.isc2.org/certifications/cissp/cissp-student-glossary.

- **Risk management:** Risk management refers to coordinating activities that direct and control the organization in terms of risk. Cybersecurity risk management activities should exhibit some level of coordination.

- **Risk appetite:** Risk appetite refers to the amount of risk that an organization is willing to accept to achieve its objectives.[9] Senior management sets the organization's cybersecurity risk appetite, typically based on the perceived benefit of assuming cybersecurity risks.

- **Risk tolerance:** Risk tolerance is the acceptable deviation from the set risk level. This means that the organization may allow some deviations from the cybersecurity risk appetite levels in pursuit of objectives at any given time. Developments in the organization's cybersecurity operating environment primarily affect its cybersecurity risk tolerance.

- **Risk profile:** The organization's risk profile refers to a comprehensive analysis of its possible risks, including cybersecurity risks. In coming up with a cybersecurity risk profile, an organization should undertake surveys of its various cybersecurity operations considering several aspects, such as the location of its cybersecurity assets, the value of those assets, stability of the countries where its data centers are located, public perceptions of its cybersecurity operations, and similar aspects.

- **Key risk indicators (KRIs):** KRIs for the cybersecurity environment refer to metrics that alert the organization and inform its management of impending cybersecurity risks. These typically use ratings and sophisticated algorithms and are forward-looking in their approach.

---

9. ISACA. "Risk Appetite vs. Risk Tolerance: What Is the Difference?" Accessed September 23, 2024. https://www.isaca.org

- **Key performance indicators (KPIs):** Cybersecurity KPIs assist the organization in understanding the cybersecurity risks that have happened in the organization's cybersecurity environment. Such risks have already affected the organization and have been acted upon. In contrast to KRIs, KPIs are in a traditional environment and follow the four main phases. Therefore, they are backward-looking in approach.

2.2.2 Cyber Risk Management Process

The cyber risk management process is the same as the risk management process in the traditional environment and follows four main phases, as shown in Figure 2.2 below.

Figure 2.2 Cybersecurity Risk Management Process

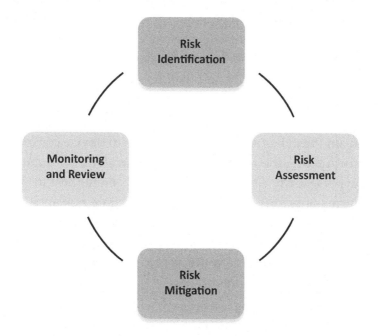

- **Risk identification:** This is the first stage in the cybersecurity risk management process and entails identifying all risks likely to affect an organization's cybersecurity posture. The risk identification process should ensure that all risks have been identified because failure to recognize all risks at this stage will mean that such risks will not be subjected to analysis and other subsequent risk management steps. The cyber risk identification process thus allows the organization to determine the extent of its attack surface accurately.

- **Risk assessment:** The risk assessment stage is concerned with analyzing the scope of each identified cybersecurity risk in terms of the likelihood of it occurring and the potential impact it would have if it happened. In the cybersecurity environment, the possibility of cybersecurity risks is typically based on the threats to the environment, the vulnerabilities within the environment, and the resultant consequences of these vulnerabilities being exploited. After their assessment, the cybersecurity risks are ranked based on their impact severity and likelihood of actualizing.

- **Risk mitigation:** During the cyber risk mitigation stage, the organization will use the information obtained from the cyber risk assessment stage to devise controls for treating the risks. Treatment often starts with the cybersecurity risk factors that have been highest in terms of priority, then moves to moderate risk and finally low-ranked risks. The cyber risk mitigation controls are varied and can be preventive, detective, or corrective, and these controls are implemented within the control environment.

- **Continuous monitoring and review:** The final stage in the cybersecurity risk management process concerns the assessment of the implemented mitigatory controls. The security controls implemented in the risk mitigation stage are monitored and assessed to determine their design and operating effectiveness. Controls are reviewed to determine if they are producing the desired outcome, reducing the cybersecurity risks to acceptable levels.

2.2.3 Common Cybersecurity Risks

To accurately perform a cybersecurity risk assessment, the organization, guided by the cybersecurity security professional, should first be aware of the broad types of cyber risk associated with the cybersecurity environment. Table 2.1 shows some of the risks.

Table 2.1 Common Cybersecurity Risks

Type of cybersecurity risk	Description
Operation risk	This risk is caused by the lack of visibility of the organization's infrastructure and data due to its cybersecurity operational activities. This may lead the organization to fail to detect attackers and cybercriminals within its networks.
Security risk	These risks are generally cybersecurity-specific and prevalent in the cybersecurity environment. They affect the cybersecurity infrastructure and cybersecurity data. The major cybersecurity risks you should take note of include credential theft, misconfiguration, overprovisioning of access, and weak access controls.

Type of cybersecurity risk	Description
Compliance risk	Compliance risk arises from an organization's non-adherence to its various legal, regulatory, and other cybersecurity requirements. The risk can result in fines and penalties being levied. You should also understand the legal and regulatory landscape of the jurisdictions you operate from. For example, if you do business with European and Canadian citizens, abiding by the General Data Protection Regulation (GDPR) and the Personal Information Protection and Electronic Documents Act (PIDEDA) respectively is key.
Supplier risk	Supplier risk is the risk that results from the organization's interactions with its suppliers. The cybersecurity environment has infrastructures that different suppliers usually provide. These suppliers may provide insecure hardware and software components, which can serve as an attack vector that attackers can exploit when introduced into the cybersecurity environment.
Reputational risk	Reputational risk arises from the hostile perception customers and other stakeholders may have regarding the organization.[10] The organization may lose its reputation because of cyber-attacks or how it handles cyber incidents. For example, suppose the organization cannot implement adequate security controls and suffers a cyber breach affecting its customers' privacy. In that case, it may suffer from a bad reputation for failing to adequately protect customers' privacy. This may lead to losing current and potential customers as they fear privacy.

2.2.4 Managing Cybersecurity Risks

An organisation can deploy various options to manage cybersecurity risk, including risk avoidance, risk transfer, risk mitigation, and risk acceptance, as explained below.

---

10. "Basel Framework." Accessed September 23, 2024. https://www.bis.org

- **Risk avoidance:** Risk avoidance is not considered a good option for managing cybersecurity risks in an organization, but it is sometimes chosen. The method involves the organization usually carrying out a cost-benefit analysis when faced with a particular type of cybersecurity risk. A risk-averse organization may decide not to carry out the project or activity when the cost outweighs the benefits.

- **Risk transfer:** Organizations that do not want to assume all the risks associated with operating in the cybersecurity environment may choose the risk transfer strategy. The organization partners with an entity, which then assumes some portions of the risk if it were to occur. An example is insurance, wherein the risk is transferred to the insurer if you take out an insurance policy.

- **Risk mitigation:** The risk method refers to the risk management practice that seeks to reduce cybersecurity risks to acceptable levels consistent with the organization's overall risk appetite. This risk reduction is achieved through establishing and implementing security controls, also known as countermeasures.

- **Risk acceptance:** In risk acceptance, the organization chooses to do nothing about the identified risks and, therefore, accepts them. This is typically pursued after performing a cost-benefit analysis, in which the organization determines that the risks identified are minimal compared to the benefits likely to be realized and that the risks are within the organization's risk appetite. The organization then proceeds with the activity or project without taking any action on the risks.

2.2.5 Benefits of Effective Cybersecurity Risk Management

As this discussion shows, there are several benefits to implementing effective cybersecurity risk management practices so that the organization can reap the resultant benefits. The following are some of the benefits:

- **Improved cybersecurity:** Implementing a process to properly identify and assess the possible risks within the cybersecurity environment can improve overall cybersecurity in organizations. This is because it allows for the implementation of appropriate security policies and controls to mitigate cybersecurity risks.

- **Increased compliance:** Cybersecurity risk management also allows the organization to improve its compliance levels. The ongoing monitoring of a comprehensive cybersecurity risk management strategy enables the organization to determine the cybersecurity aspects that fall short of compliance requirements and reconfigure them accordingly.

- **Proactive cybersecurity:** Cybersecurity risk management encourages the organization to respond proactively to cyber-attacks while also allowing the organization to stay prepared for future cyber incidents. By prioritizing some risks, the security teams will get an understanding of the risks that should be addressed first, thus protecting the organization from the most severe cyber risks.

- **Reduced costs:** The cybersecurity risk assessment process can assist the organization in reducing its risk profile, hence reducing the costs associated with those risks if they were to occur. There are also costs associated with non-compliance, such as fines and penalties, that can also be reduced through the implementation of a sound cybersecurity risk management program.

2.3 Cybersecurity Compliance

Cybersecurity compliance refers to adhering to cybersecurity requirements as set forth by relevant authoritative bodies. These requirements may take the form of standards, regulations, or statutes. Often, noncompliance may lead to organizations incurring heavy penalties in the form of fines, hence the need to always adhere to the requirements.

Regardless of the cybersecurity framework(s) the organization must comply with, certain best practices can be followed to achieve successful compliance. The cybersecurity security professional should have an appreciation of such best practices to be well-paced to advise the organization and offer the necessary support throughout the compliance process including the following.

- **Determine the applicable framework(s):** The first stage is for the organization to determine the cybersecurity compliance frameworks it must comply with to meet its customers' security requirements. The organization can also comply with more than one framework, as most frameworks consist of overlapping controls.

- **Develop a clear cybersecurity policy:** The organization should develop a cybersecurity policy in line with or referencing the adopted framework. The policy can be a stand-alone policy or incorporated into the master information security policy. A clear policy assists the organization in implementing and maintaining the framework it adopts.

- **Identify relevant compliance requirements:** The organization, assisted by the cybersecurity professional, should identify specific compliance requirements for implementation from the cybersecurity policy and the compliance framework itself. These requirements can then be allocated to different teams for implementation and/or observance.

- **Train and educate employees:** The organization should invest in training and educating its employees on the various requirements of the cybersecurity compliance framework and what is expected of them. To achieve this, the organization should be prepared to provide training materials and other requirements and convene workshops to ensure everyone is onboarded on the cybersecurity compliance processes.

- **Carry out regular audits:** The organization should carry out regular audits during implementation to ensure the implementation process progresses well or after implementation and certification to ensure the cybersecurity requirements continue to be maintained. The audits should analyze the current cybersecurity environment against the adopted compliance framework.

2.4 Cybersecurity Compliance Frameworks

Cybersecurity compliance frameworks guide organizations in implementing controls to enhance the security posture of cybersecurity environments. Several frameworks can be adopted, and each organization has the freedom to choose a relevant framework. Table 2.2 below details some of the most common compliance frameworks applicable to cybersecurity.

Table 2.2 Common Cybersecurity Compliance Frameworks

Compliance framework	Description
ISO/IEC 27001:2022	ISO/IEC 27001: 2022 is an information security management standard developed by the International Organization for Standardization (ISO), a nongovernmental international organization dedicated to developing and publishing standards for use by various organizations worldwide. The purpose of ISO/IEC 27001:2022 is to provide a framework for establishing, implementing, maintaining, and improving an information security management system (ISMS).[11] The primary benefit of using this standard in the cybersecurity environment is that it is vendor and technology-neutral and can be applied in various environments and technological settings.
ISO 27017:2015	ISO 27017: 2015 provides guidelines for implementing cybersecurity controls.[12] It presents a code of best practices that suppliers and cybersecurity customers alike can adopt in all aspects of cybersecurity security. It extends ISO 27001: 2022 but is designed for cybersecurity environments and services. The standard is often preferred for its emphasis on distinguishing between the security aspects of cybersecurity and the risks associated with cybersecurity services and its focus on privacy concerns arising out of operating in cybersecurity.

---

11. 14:00-17:00. "ISO/IEC 27001:2022." ISO. Accessed September 23, 2024. https://www.iso.org
12. 14:00-17:00. "ISO/IEC 27017:2015." ISO. Accessed September 23, 2024. https://www.iso.org

Compliance framework	Description
SOC	System and Organization Controls (SOC) reporting is a suite of audit reports that assure financial reporting and security controls, including cybersecurity security controls. The American Institute of CPA (AICPA) focuses on the design and operating effectiveness of internal controls for organizations that provide services to other entities and provides the reporting framework. The main SOC reports relevant to cybersecurity are: • **SOC 1:** An SOC 1 report evaluates the organization's financial reporting controls. It is not very useful for assessing the cybersecurity environment as it does not deal with information security aspects. It is designed for other stakeholders, such as investors. • **SOC 2:** These audit reports provide results of an organization's information systems in terms of security, availability, processing integrity, confidentiality, and privacy (known as the trusted criteria) and are the most relevant reports for organizations operating in cybersecurity.
PCI DSS	The Payment Card Industry Data Encryption Standard (PCI DSS) is a compliance standard that applies to organizations that operate in the cybersecurity environment and handle credit card transactions. The major credit card companies established it and its requirements for all organizations dealing with credit cards. The standard comprises four (4) levels, ranging from level 1 to level 4, depending on the number of transactions processed per year.

Compliance framework	Description
NIST	The National Institute of Standards and Technology (NIST) is a US federal agency that provides several standards and guidelines for public use addressing cybersecurity and other aspects of information security. The most relevant standards that can be adopted include the NIST cybersecurity framework v2.0 (CSF v2.0)[13], which provides guidelines, standards, and practices to address cybersecurity issues in an organization. The framework consists of five (5) aspects, as explained below: • **Govern:** deals with establishing an organization's cybersecurity risk management strategy. • **Identify:** addresses the identification of cybersecurity-related risks to achieve compliance. • **Protect:** implements a set of security controls to achieve cybersecurity. • **Detect:** establishes measures to detect cybersecurity events and irregularities. • **Respond:** Implement cybersecurity response plans.

---

13. Nist, Gaithersburg Md. "The NIST Cybersecurity Framework 2.0." Gaithersburg, MD: National Institute of Standards and Technology, 2023. https://doi.org/10.6028/NIST.CSWP.29.

Compliance framework	Description
CSA STAR	The Cybersecurity Security Alliance (CSA)'s security, trust, assurance, and risk (star) are some of the most common robust cybersecurity security frameworks that can be pursued to protect the cybersecurity environment. It comprises several processes and principles, including transparency, rigorous auditing, and harmonizing cybersecurity standards. The method includes assessment, third-party audits, and continuous monitoring for the organization to achieve and maintain compliance.
CSA Cybersecurity Controls Matrix (CCM)	Also, from the CSA, the cybersecurity controls matrix (CCM) v4.0[14] includes nearly 200 control objectives and related control requirements that are divided into some 17 cybersecurity security domains that align with standards such as ISO/IEC 27001: 2022, PCI DSS v4.0 and NIST CSF.2.0. Organizations operating in cybersecurity can use a model and create a list of the requirements that are specified in the matrix and decide which ones to comply with.
Center for Internet Security (CIS) controls	The CIS framework is published by the Center for Internet Security (CIS), an organization that provides a set of security best practices for cybersecurity. The framework provides several critical security controls that, if implemented in cybersecurity environments, can significantly reduce cybersecurity risks. By implementing the CIS Control Framework, cybersecurity organizations can improve their security posture while also simplifying compliance requirements.

---

14. Puma Rajapruek, Nuttapong, and Twittie Senivongse. "Classifying Cloud Provider Security Conformance to Cloud Controls Matrix." In *2014 11th International Joint Conference on Computer Science and Software Engineering (JCSSE)*, 268–73. Chon Buri: IEEE, 2014. https://doi.org/10.1109/JCSSE.2014.6841879.

Chapter Summary

- Cybersecurity governance, risk, and compliance (GRC) is a vital process for organizations to assess the effectiveness and efficiency of their cybersecurity governance practices.

- By evaluating compliance with regulations, assessing its performance and efficiency, and focusing on critical areas of governance, organizations can optimize their cybersecurity investments, mitigate risks, align cybersecurity strategies with business objectives, and measure performance.

- Cybersecurity GRC provides valuable insights into an organization's cybersecurity governance, risk and compliance, and opportunities for improvement.

- By considering cybersecurity GRC in the overall governance structures, organizations can continuously enhance their cybersecurity governance practices, strengthen their cybersecurity posture, and drive business success.

Quiz

1. Your organization is implementing an Information Security Management System (ISMS) to improve its cybersecurity posture. Which framework should you recommend for this exercise?
   a. COBIT19
   b. POPIA
   c. ISO/IEC 27001
   d. CCM.

2. Why is the implementation of cybersecurity governance crucial for modern organizations?
   a. It controls IT costs.
   b. It provides a standardized way to manage cybersecurity risks.
   c. It enhances the formulation of profit strategies.
   d. Furthermore, it eliminates operational risks.

3. As a cybersecurity professional, why do you regularly conduct cyber risk assessments?
   a. To identify, analyze, and mitigate threats and vulnerabilities.
   b. To enhance profitability
   c. To cut down on the number of audits
   d. To eliminate all cybersecurity risks

4. You are a cyber risk specialist at your organization and have been asked to lead a cyber risk assessment team. When carrying out the risk assessment, which of the following would you consider to determine the potential impact of a cybersecurity threat?
   a. Reputational damage
   b. Competitor actions
   c. Employee dissatisfaction
   d. Reduced expansion capabilities.

5. Why would you implement a cyber risk register?
   a. To document identified risks and mitigation measures
   b. To track risk performance
   c. To avoid all cyber risks
   d. To eliminate all risks

6. How does the integration of cybersecurity GRC functions benefit an organization involved in the development of software?
   a. It streamlines related processes
   b. It improved the company's profitability levels.
   c. It enhances job satisfaction among developers.
   d. It results in a reduced ability to treat risks.

7. A new cybersecurity law has been promulgated that affects your organization's operations. Which of the following actions will ensure compliance?
   a. Conduct a gap analysis and align existing policies.
   b. Increase the budget for the security departments.
   c. Adjust reporting relationship in the security department.
   d. Ignore the new law, as cybersecurity laws always change.

8. During a cybersecurity audit, it was discovered that several potential risks were not identified in the initial risk identification stage. As a cybersecurity specialist, you should advise your organization that:
   a. The risks will be automatically mitigated
   b. The risks will not be subjected to the entire process of risk assessment
   c. The risks will be more severe
   d. The risks will be more easily managed

9. An organization conducts a cybersecurity risk assessment and discovers that a particular cyber risk has a high likelihood but low impact. How would you rank such a risk?
   a. High-priority
   b. Moderate priority
   c. Very Low priority
   d. No priority

10. After carrying out a cybersecurity risk assessment, you advise an organization to implement preventive controls. Which of the following represents the stage you are at in the cybersecurity risk management process?
    a. Risk detection
    b. Risk identification
    c. Risk mitigation
    d. Risk evaluation

Answers

1 – c	2 – b	3 – a	4 – a	5 – a
6 – a	7 – a	8 – c	9 – b	10 – c

Self-Learning Management Series

Chapter 3
Physical Security

> **Key Learning Objectives**
> - Various forms of access controls that can be implemented to enhance physical security
> - Critical physical security threats that can affect organizations
> - Essential physical security measures that should be implemented to address the identified security threats
> - Awareness of challenges in implementing physical security solutions
> - Measures that can be taken to limit and control the exposure of certain physical assets to threats

Physical security involves protecting people, property, data, and computing assets from physical actions that can cause their damage or loss. This includes preventing theft, vandalism, accidental damage, natural elements, burglary, and terrorism. Physical security is, therefore, a crucial element in the overall cybersecurity architecture.

3.1 Access Control

Within the context of physical security, access control is a security discipline that encompasses all those processes an organization puts in place to control physical access to its information systems. This is vital in protecting assets physically and also assists in the protection of the information assets that reside in or traverse the physical information systems environment.

3.1.1 Access Control Methods

There are various examples of access control methods that organizations can choose from. The cybersecurity professional should, however, note that these access control measures can vary significantly in terms of method, approach, and cost. Standard methods include the following:

- **Buildings:** Buildings often serve as the first line of defense for most physical security systems, followed by other related security features such as fences, gates, walls, and doors that also serve as physical deterrents to criminal entry. Buildings can also be enhanced; other security measures such as locks, barbed wire, fencing, lights, and warning signs reduce the number of casual attempts carried out by cybercriminals. Therefore, organizations must regularly assess their buildings as part of their regular physical security risk assessment processes. It is also critical to consider security measures for new buildings and sites as early as possible, especially during the concept and design stages, to site and implement hardening against natural disasters.
- **Security guards:** Security guards are also an effective access control method. They come in as a deterrent measure against entry-level attackers. The primary

reason for the preference of security guards is their discriminating effect, in that they can decide based on the situations prevailing, unlike other methods, which do not have a human element.

- **ID card scanners:** ID card scanners represent one of the most advanced access control methods. Alongside other sophisticated technologies, such as near-field communication (NFC), ID cards can provide physical authentication capabilities that cybersecurity teams can use to verify the identities of individuals entering and exiting various information processing facilities.
- **Surveillance:** Surveillance is a crucial security element for prevention and post-incident recovery. It refers to the technology, personnel, and resources organizations use to monitor real-world locations for security threats. The most common forms of surveillance include CCTV, patrol guards, sensors, alarms, and other notification systems. The significant advantage of surveillance systems is their ability to capture criminal behavior as they prevent it. Another key benefit is their ability to provide evidence for the commission of cybercrime.[15]
- **Keyless access control:** With the implementation of keyless access control, users do not need to carry a physical credential that can be easily lost, misplaced, or copied. Instead, they simply input a Personal Identification Number (PIN) keypad lock to gain access to physical facilities. This reduces the risk of lost or duplicated keys. Commercial door keypad lock devices require a dedicated power source and are often configured to communicate using internet connections. This allows

---

15. Koziarski, Jacek, and Jin Ree Lee. "Connecting Evidence-Based Policing and Cybercrime," March 2, 2020. https://www.crimrxiv.com

system administrators to monitor, adjust, and manage the network remotely using smart devices.

- **Video technology:** Video technology consists of access control units that include two-way video. With this added layer of verification, access control systems administrators can check people attempting to enter physical facilities. The significant advantage of video technology is its ability to use innovative technology that connects to either the cloud or to a web interface for easier administration. Therefore, an organization can monitor and control its entry points and collect valuable data for further analysis.

- **Sensor technology:** With sensor technology, an organization can detect environmental changes and alert security teams to potential threats that need countermeasures. Sensors come in different forms, including smoke alarms, which help detect a fire, while other sensors detect and observe motion, sounds, light, vaping, temperature, etc. Upon detecting these, the sensors notify the operators and enable the security team to respond quickly. Sensors can also be integrated with the broader physical security setup, permitting operators to gain greater visibility of the incidents. Operators can undertake system lockdowns through the access control system if necessary. Providing quick alerts and fast response sensors can assist cybersecurity personnel in mitigating threats and restoring safe environments for computing systems.

3.1.2 Importance of Access Control

Access control is an essential element of any security-conscious organization's physical security architecture because of its many benefits. These benefits include.

- **Prevents unauthorized access:** The primary objective of access control is to prevent unauthorized access and safeguard an organization's physical assets from attacks. It should, however, be noted that the design of access control measures should not impede the provision of access to those authorized. Access should ideally be provisioned using the Principle of Least Privilege (POLP). The POLP mandates the provisioning of only the required access to perform the required tasks and nothing more, thus reducing the attack surface.

- **Generates logs and trails:** Access control assists organizations in maintaining an audit trail of access. This includes information area accesses, entities that accessed or attempted to access critical areas, the time when the access happened, and so forth. This makes access control an effective method of discouraging unauthorized users while creating a forensic-friendly data environment. An organization can track its asset activity using multiple failed login attempts and attempted access. Figure 3.1 shows a typical example of log aggregation.

Figure 3.1 Log Aggregation

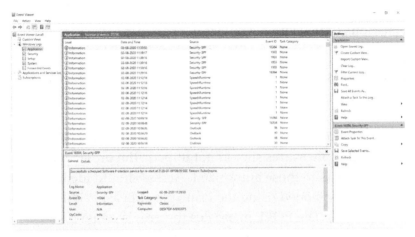

Source: https://www.logsign.com/blog/logging-of-security-events-in-siem/

- **Supports a risk-based approach:** One of the most effective ways to optimize physical security is to adopt a risk-based approach and evaluate scenarios based on one's risk profile. Those areas that are considered riskier will be protected with more sophisticated access controls than areas considered less risky.

- **Promotes accountability:** By tying access control to individuals and introducing audit trails, access controls have been assisting organizations in improving their visibility over personnel activity and ensuring employees and other stakeholders are accountable for their activities.

3.2 Physical Security Risks, Threats, and Vulnerabilities

3.2.1 Physical Security Risks and Threats

While each organization's physical security risks may differ, cybersecurity professionals should be aware of some common physical security threats. These include the following physical risks and threats:

- **Unauthorized access/entry:** This is the most common threat facing physical security measures. Unauthorized access can be perpetrated in various ways in the physical environment. Standard methods include tailgating, social engineering, or gaining access using stolen credentials. Unauthorized access is undesirable because once an attacker gets access or entry into a facility, the possibilities for damage are limitless. In most cases, once attackers gain entry or access, it's only a matter of when and not if the other more damaging physical security threats begin to occur.

- **Theft:** Theft is another physical security risk, especially for businesses that own many valuable assets, from equipment to data assets. Organizations that keep valuable assets on their premises are vulnerable to theft. For high-value assets, physical assets can also be associated with burglary.

- **Damage:** Organizations are always at risk of their property being destroyed or tampered with by malicious attackers. Damage to physical property can come from many angles, such as sabotage by insiders, especially disgruntled employees, or vandalism, which takes more of an ideological position. Therefore, an organization must prevent damage and protect its assets and data on its technology assets.

- **Violence and terrorist acts:** This form of threat is associated with acts of aggression and altercations that can threaten an establishment and the safety of its people. State actors target computer-controlled infrastructure, such as nuclear facilities that usually ferment it. War, harassment, cyberattacks, and targeted violence are all physical security threats commonly found in the cybersecurity landscape.

- **Insider threats:** These are threats to physical security from inside the organization. They pose significant risks to the organization's physical security posture as they come from within the organization and are perpetrated by people with knowledge of the internal control systems and how they work. As a result, insiders can easily circumvent controls, making detecting and preventing them challenging. Insider threats come from various sources, such as current or former employees, suppliers, contractors, or business partners. Motivations for attacks include obtaining financial gain, effective revenge, and espionage. Some insider threats may also be caused by unintentional negligence and a lack of security awareness.

- **Natural disasters:** Physical computing facilities also face threats from natural disasters. These can be devastating to organizations. Natural disasters come from various sources, including earthquakes, hurricanes, cyclones, and wildfires. They can cause massive destruction to physical computing facilities when they strike. Organizations, therefore, need to strengthen their physical infrastructure to withstand the effects of natural disasters.

3.2.2 Physical Security Vulnerabilities

Physical security vulnerabilities are loopholes or weaknesses within the organization that lead to exposure to physical threats. They include the following:

- **Negligence:** Mistakes and carelessness, especially by insiders, can damage an organization's physical security posture. Employees may leave secure areas open or unlocked or lose keys or other security requirements required for accessing secure areas. All these can lead to security attacks as cybercriminals take advantage of the vulnerabilities to gain access.

- **Improper security implementations:** In some cases, an organization may implement improper physical security implementations, including installing improper access controls. Improper access controls mean that the controls are not fit for their purpose, which gives an organization a false sense of security. Sophisticated attackers can test the security systems as a preliminary act to a major attack. If they find weaknesses due to improper access controls, a significant attack can be carried out with devastating consequences for the organization.

- **Malicious insiders:** Another physical security vulnerability is the presence of attackers within an organization. This can significantly threaten an organization's physical security posture and is a direct risk, as insiders consistently succeed in their attacks. Malicious insiders can steal physical computing assets and tamper with credentials to obtain access. Others can collaborate with outside actors to cause harm to an organization's physical infrastructure. This includes providing sensitive security information, including how to bypass controls.

- **Equipment failure:** Equipment failure is a significant vulnerability that can lead to successful attacks on an organization's physical infrastructure. It creates vulnerabilities when there is a break, especially in the operation of access controls. For example, power outages may render access controls down, thus leaving security gaps that attackers can exploit.

3.2.3 Management of Physical Threats and Vulnerabilities

Maintaining an organization's people, information, and assets secure involves ongoing activity to detect and manage evolving threats and vulnerabilities. To manage an organization's vulnerabilities in its physical security, take the following action:

- **Develop and implement a physical security policy:** An organization should develop a policy to guide its physical security activities. The policy will specify all the organization's physical security expectations, ranging from the provisioning and use of identities and authentication systems to how to handle cybersecurity incidents, including the reporting responsibilities of employees. Disciplinary actions should also be stated for failing to comply with the requirements as stated in the policy.

- **Implement an incident response process:** An organization should be able to implement the incident response aspects of its physical security system. This ensures the organization can respond effectively and promptly to physical threats it may be exposed to.[16] The Incident Response Plan (IRP) should be developed and implemented, while an Incident Response Team (IRT) should be set up to handle physical incidents. Other aspects of the incident-handling process, such as establishing points of contact and recovery, should also be considered. For a detailed discussion on IRP, refer to Chapter Nine.

- **Perform regular risk assessments:** Being proactive in physical security entails staying on top of physical threats and vulnerabilities or weaknesses that may affect an organization's operations. This is achieved by performing regular risk assessments around its physical security posture. The risk assessment can inform an organization of the physical security controls to be implemented. The approval of any physical security investment in any organization should be based on the risk assessment results. In addition, the risk assessment process should allow the organization to adapt its physical security controls in response to identified risks.

- **Invest in an on-site Security Operations Center (SOC):** An organization should analyze all factors and decide whether to monitor its physical infrastructure in-house or outsource it to a physical security company. One primary consideration is whether the organization has enough space on-site for an SOC. Outsourcing the SOC can relieve some operational pressure on the internal security team. However, the organization should ensure that its physical security policies require the outsourcer to keep its data secure.

---

16. Edwards, Dr. Jason. "Incident Response Management." In *Critical Security Controls for Effective Cyber Defense: A Comprehensive Guide to CIS 18 Controls*, edited by Dr. Jason Edwards, 497–526. Berkeley, CA: Apress, 2024. https://doi.org/10.1007/979-8-8688-0506-6_17.

- **Perform regular penetration tests:** While penetration tests are mainly associated with logical access controls, they are also recommended for physical infrastructure. Investment in penetration tests will assist organizations in identifying and understanding the vulnerabilities available in their physical infrastructure. Measures can then be implemented to address the security loopholes and improve the security posture.
- **Invest in redundancy:** Redundancy allows an organization to be resilient in the face of physical attacks. This should be aided by a Business Continuity/Disaster Recovery (BCDR) Plan. The BC/DR Plan helps guide the organization in implementing redundancy. This ensures that when the physical infrastructure is affected by a cyber-attack, it can quickly recover and ensure continuity of operations.

3.3 Physical Security Controls

Physical security controls include all the security measures implemented to protect information assets from physical damage. They involve securing and protecting organizational assets from harm due to physical events such as natural disasters like fires and floods, as well as human-inflicted risks such as data theft or sabotage and vandalism of information assets. Physical security controls fall into four broad categories: deter, detect, delay, and respond, as shown in Figure 3.2 below.

Figure 3.2 Levels of Physical Security Control

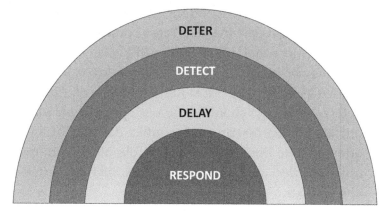

Source: https://www.btigroup.com

According to Figure 3.2 above, these different layers of physical security methods work together to achieve overall security. These levels of physical security begin with deter located at the outermost level, then proceed inwards to the detect level until reaching the responding level. This is explained below.

- **Deter:** Deterrence in physical security measures focuses on keeping intruders and attackers out of the secured physical facility.[17] This is achieved by deploying perimeter security elements such as fences and barbed wire. Clear warning signs stating that the physics facility has robust security controls can also deter criminals. However, deterrence may not be the best for the more sophisticated and daring attackers; they can find ways to violate the security controls and proceed to attack. This is especially true when the deterrence controls are not strong enough to stop attackers.

---

17. Pelco. "What Is Physical Security? Policies, Measures & Examples." Accessed September 28, 2024. https://www.pelco.com

- **Detect:** The objective of detection is to catch intruders if they disregard the security controls or get past ineffective deterrence controls. Criminals use various methods to get past the deterrence controls, especially the deterrence measures mentioned above. For example, they may be behind an authorized employee, a practice known as tailgating, or just find another way. Adequate detective controls should be able to spot the intruder quickly before they proceed to inflict damage. CCTVs often fall into this category of controls, along with many other physical access control systems, such as alarms and sensors.

- **Delay:** The delay category consists of those controls that delay the movement of attackers with the hope that they can be caught or to provide the organization sufficient time to come up with a proper response strategy to the attack. However, in physical security, it is rare to find a control solely dedicated to the delay function. Several physical security systems combine delay with detection and deterrence categories. For example, access control systems require credentials to open locked doors. This serves many purposes, deterring entry and slowing an intruder down so that it becomes easier for him or her to be apprehended.

- **Respond/deny:** This is the stage where the organization uses the technology available to respond to intruders and cybercriminals. The goal is to deny damage to information systems by the attacker, hence, the response phase is sometimes known as the deny category. Physical security response activities can take many forms, including communication systems, security guards, designated first responders, and processes and procedures for locking down a site and alerting law enforcement if required. Responding to physical threats is critical for organizations but is often overlooked in cybersecurity. Failure to respond effectively to physical threats can lead to enormous losses for the organization and affect the organization's business continuity capabilities.

Cybersecurity professionals should know that some physical security systems have multiple roles: they can deter, detect, and delay, while others can also respond.

Table 3.1 is a typical summary of some IT physical controls that can be implemented in an organization.

Table 3.1 Examples of IT Physical Controls

Control	Description
Physical access controls	These control entry to organizational computing facilities and movements happening within such facilities. These include: • Locking doors • Alarms • Fences • Barriers
Hardware security	Hardware security controls physical equipment (e.g., computers, printers, and scanners) used to handle and process sensitive data. This includes: • Regular updates • Patches (System and software updates for fixing security vulnerabilities in a product)

Control	Description
Security perimeters	Security perimeters are deployed to establish physical boundaries for buildings or areas for controlling access. This includes: • Fences • Walls • Gates • Surveillance cameras
Visitor management	Visitor management allows an organization to track and manage visitors entering the organization's premises and information processing facilities.[18] Examples of visitor management activities include: • Sign-in procedures • Badges • Escort policies
Biometric authentication	These make use of unique physical traits and improved security beyond traditional passwords. These include: • Fingerprints • Retina scans • Face recognition • Voice recognition
Environmental controls	Environmental controls assist in maintaining optimal ecological conditions for the organization's IT equipment and help prevent environmental damage. Examples include: • Humidity levels • Temperature levels

---

18. Burton, Lou. "What Is a Visitor Management System? Everything You Need to Know." Accessed September 28, 2024. https://www.swipedon.com

Control	Description
Secure disposal procedures	Secure disposal procedures ensure the proper disposal of sensitive organizational materials, data, and information stored on physical storage media. Examples include: • Wiping • Overwriting

3.4 Physical Security Challenges

Implementing physical security controls in organizations has its challenges. However, it is critical for the concerned organizations to devise strategies to address the obstacles to allow for the smooth implementation and operation of the various physical security controls. Challenges typically encountered include the following:

- **Funds shortages:** Lack of adequate funds prevents many businesses from making an appropriate level of physical security investment. This is compounded by the fact that some physical security measures are very costly and can exhaust existing budgetary capabilities. This is especially true with modern video, CCTVs, and sensor technology. In making decisions regarding allocating funds toward implementing physical security measures, the organization should seek to strike a balance. Failure to deploy the necessary measures can result in even more costs for the organization when threats strike without adequate protection. It is important to note that the cost of any security measure should not exceed the value of the assets that are to be protected. Therefore, if you are a small business, you may opt to implement the following cost-effective physical security measures:

- Training employees in good cybersecurity principles and cyber hygiene
- Keeping devices, software, and applications updated
- Securing physical assets with good password practices
- Limiting physical access through perimeter security such as fences
- Providing adequate lighting during the night to deter intruders

- **Skills shortages:** The current global shortage of cybersecurity professionals is another challenge facing organizations in implementing physical security measures. Even when the organization has managed to procure advanced technological systems, they are usually useless when there are not enough skilled personnel to operate and manage them. Organizations should, therefore, increase their training budgets to address internal cybersecurity skills gaps and manage their physical environments effectively.

- **Lack of integration:** Integration enhances organizational security; however, the physical security posture can be affected if various security controls are not adequately integrated into a more significant physical security architecture. Therefore, it is critical for an organization to thoroughly understand each physical security control system and its interfaces, and how they feed information and interact with each other. Integration with logical security systems is also crucial in enhancing the organization's security posture. It is therefore critical to ensure that the physical access security processes in place complement logical access controls (for example, secure server rooms can be designed to protect credentials).

- **Logistical challenges:** Physical security controls and their management can be logistical, especially when an organization secures large areas. This is compounded by the fact that no two or more sites are the same, and managing physical sites may need many strategies and action plans. Therefore, the organization should be flexible enough to adjust to different environments when implementing physical security measures.
- **Inadequate physical security planning:** Effective deployment and management of physical security measures require the organization to draw up physical security plans, which in turn require extensive input from organizational units and other stakeholders. This planning is necessary as physical security measures do not occur in a vacuum, but they ultimately affect the day-to-day operations of an organization. This, therefore, means that the organization should use adequate planning systems to manage its physical infrastructure. This will lead to well-researched physical security plans that can cover the whole organization holistically.
- **Tailgating and social engineering:** Physical security controls also suffer from the twin challenges of tailgating and social engineering. Tailgating is where an intruder can get unauthorized entry by following an authorized person. You should therefore stay alert to such incidences to avoid breaches.

Chapter Summary

- Physical security is fundamental to an organization's security effectiveness and should be considered an important part of the organization's overall cybersecurity architecture.
- Access control is an effective method of protecting an organization's physical computing assets by restricting and controlling access to its premises and information processing facilities.
- An organization should implement relevant and manageable physical security measures.
- The deter, detect, delay, and response method is tried and tested to implement physical security controls. It starts with deterrence, works inwards to detection, progresses further to delay, and finally responds to physical threats.
- Organizations face several challenges in implementing physical security measures, including budgetary constraints, skills shortages, and poor planning.
- An organization should implement complementary physical security measures to successfully protect its people and physical computing assets.
- The best way to guarantee a safe and secure workplace is to carefully observe what an organization needs and then find the right physical security tools, technology, and methods for the job.

Quiz

1. A cybersecurity professional should understand the various forms of cyber-physical threats that can affect an organization. Which is not a type of physical security threat from a cybersecurity perspective?
   a. Sabotage
   b. Unauthorized entry
   c. Cross-site scripting
   d. Damage

2. Physical security controls fall into four broad categories: deter, detect, delay, and respond, as shown. Which of the following is the objective of the deter category?
   a. Prevent entry
   b. Ignore entry
   c. Detect entry
   d. Respond to entry

3. Cybersecurity professionals often encounter challenges in implementing physical security controls in organizations. Which of the following is a challenge related to people dynamics?
   a. Skills shortage
   b. Lack of integration
   c. Poor logistics
   d. Inadequate funds

4. ACC Limited is developing a physical security policy intended to protect its physical assets from cyber threats. Which of the following should form part of the policy to ensure effective implementation?
   a. Project timelines
   b. Access controls
   c. Budget allocations
   d. Software product development

5. Which risk management framework is widely used for identifying, assessing, and managing physical security risks and is used internationally?
   a. ISO/IEC 27005
   b. ISO 31000
   c. COBIT
   d. Six Sigma

6. Which of the following represents the importance of documenting all the physical controls in your organization?
   a. It helps in demonstrating compliance with requirements.
   b. It improves employee satisfaction.
   c. It enhances the effectiveness of logical controls.
   d. It is not necessary to document physical controls.

7. As a cybersecurity professional, you have identified a significant physical security risk at your organization that requires effective mitigatory measures. What would you do to mitigate this risk?
   a. Create a mitigation policy.
   b. Increase the number of security personnel.
   c. Develop and follow a mitigation plan.
   d. Perform a penetration test.

8. A cybersecurity professional should be in a position to differentiate between physical threats and vulnerabilities. Which of the following represents a physical security vulnerability?
   a. Programming errors
   b. Weaknesses within the organization
   c. Network issues
   d. Database issues

9. Which of the following is an example of negligence on the part of employees in physical security?
   a. Installing proper access controls
   b. Leaving secure areas open or unlocked
   c. Conducting regular risk assessments
   d. Leaving the office locked

10. Cybersecurity professionals should properly advise company management to ensure the proper implementation and configuration of cybersecurity solutions. Which of the following is a risk of improper security implementations and configurations?
    a. Leads to enhanced security
    b. Provide the organization with a false sense of security
    c. Improves access control
    d. Enhances compliance

Answers

1 – c	2 – a	3 – a	4 – b	5 – b
6 – a	7 – c	8 – b	9 – b	10 – b

CHAPTER 4
Network Security

Key Learning Objectives
- The various forms of network security controls that can be implemented to enhance physical security
- The importance of network security controls in the overall cybersecurity setup of an organization
- Network devices and technologies that can be deployed within an organization to enhance security
- Network security controls that should be implemented to address identified security threats
- Challenges encountered in implementing network security solutions and strategies to overcome them

Network security involves protecting data and information, maintaining shared security data, ensuring reliable access and network performance, and protecting data from cyber threats. A well-designed network security architecture assists an organization in reducing losses associated with data breaches and other security events.

4.1 Network Security Devices

Network devices are communication tools that facilitate the transmission and reception of data securely and play a crucial role in enabling seamless communication among internet-compatible electronic network devices, which are critical for establishing and managing networks. The purpose of a computer network is to facilitate the sharing of resources such as files, printers, and internet connections among users and devices in an organization. To better understand the operations and functions of various network devices, an appreciation of the Open Systems Interconnection (OSI) is crucial as it specifies how a network functions and standardizes how systems communicate.

4.1.1 The OSI Model

To better understand the operations and functions of various network devices, an appreciation of the Open Systems Interconnection (OSI) is crucial. The OSI Model specifies how a network functions and standardizes how systems communicate. The OSI Model is a generic tool supported by a wide range of device suppliers and is used for developing any network model consisting of seven (7) layers, with each layer separate from the other layers. It seeks to highlight the various network devices operating at each layer and their associated tasks. It also provides you with information regarding the types of cyber attacks that can happen at each layer to enable you to deploy the necessary controls. However, the cybersecurity professional should note that the OSI model is only a theoretical model and is used to assist you to conceptually visualise the operation of various technologies; it does not necessarily mean the referred technologies ought to be available during the time of study.

Figure 4.1 The OSI Model

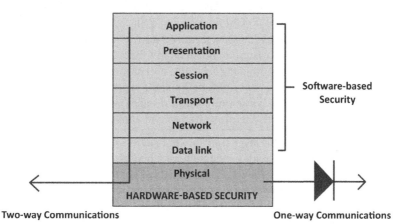

Source: https://www.avnet.com

The seven layers are explained in descending order in Table 4.1.

Table 4.1 Layers of the OSI Model

Layer	Description
Layer 7: The application layer	This layer enables the user to interact with the application and communicate effectively. This layer is the closest to the end user and acts as a window for the application services to access the network and show the received information to the user.
Layer 6: Presentation Layer	The role of the presentation layer is to translate data for the application layer based on the semantics or syntax the application will accept.[19] It also performs encryption and compression of sensitive data before transmitting it over communication channels.

---

19. "RPubs - OSI Model." Accessed October 3, 2024. https://rpubs.com

Layer	Description
Layer 5: Session Layer	The session layer sets up coordinates and ends conversations between applications. It determines how long a system will wait for another application to respond and facilitates establishing connections, maintaining sessions, and authenticating. It ensures sessions are functional during data transfer and ends communication sessions with the lower layers with the presentation and application layer.
Layer 4: Transport Layer	This layer transfers data across a network and provides capabilities such as error-checking mechanisms and data flow controls. It also performs several network management tasks, such as sequencing data packets.
Layer 3: Network Layer	The network layer transmits data into and through other networks and comprises network protocols that perform the packaging of data with correct network address information, selecting the appropriate routes. It receives frames from the data link layer and sends them to their intended destinations according to the addresses in the frame. Routers are a vital component in this layer as they route information to its intended destinations.
Layer 2: Data Link Layer	The primary purpose of the data link or protocol layer in a program is to handle moving data into and out of a physical link in a network. It addresses problems that occur because of bit transmission errors and ensures that the pace of the data flow does not overwhelm the sending and receiving devices. The data link layer comprises the following sublayers. **Logical Link Control (LLC):** The LLC multiplexes, performs flow control and acknowledgment, and notifies upper layers if transmit/receive errors occur. **Media Access Control (MAC):** The media access control tracks data frames using MAC addresses of the sending and receiving hardware. It organizes each frame, marking the starting and ending bits for each frame, which can be sent along the physical layer medium.

Layer	Description
Layer 1: Physical Layer	The physical layer transports data using electrical or procedural interfaces from one device to another along the network. It determines the setup of physical connections and data presentation for transport using the physical medium. It also performs modulation and specifies the transmission rate necessary for successful transmission. In addition, it specified the physical network topologies in a network (bus, tree, star, mesh).[20]

4.1.2 Types of Network Devices

The cybersecurity professional should be aware of the various types of network devices and their uses, which include the following:

- **Hub:** A hub connects and manages both digital and analog data when configured appropriately. A USB hub, for example, allows multiple USB devices to connect with one computer, even if that computer only has one USB connection. It operates at Layer 1 of the OSI model, is easy to install, and does not affect the performance of the network seriously. However, it is incapable of filtering traffic and, therefore, can allow malicious traffic to pass through, making it less useful for security purposes.[21]

- **Switch:** A switch is a network device that controls the flow of signals in networking. It intelligently forwards data based on hardware addresses and increases available bandwidth. A switch enables the user to open

---

20. Contributor, Staff. "What Is Network Topology? Best Guide to Types & Diagrams - DNSstuff." Software Reviews, Opinions, and Tips - DNSstuff, August 15, 2019. https://www.dnsstuff.com
21. Motadata. "Network Devices: Importance, Functions and Types." Accessed October 3, 2024. https://www.motadata.com

or close a connection and keeps an address list of all its connected devices. A network switch is much more advanced than a hub but is not as advanced as a router and operates at the Data Link layer (Layer 2) of the OSI model. However, switches are costly, and broadcast traffic can be problematic.

- **Router:** A router examines incoming packets to determine the correct target IP address and sends the packet to that address. Routers can filter and forward data, store network information, and play a vital role in controlling and optimizing network traffic. Routers typically connect LANs and WANs and use a rapidly updating routing table to make routing decisions for data packets. They operate at Layer 3 of the OSI model. However, they analyse data from Layers 1 to 3. A router can connect various network architectures and reduce network traffic by establishing collision domains and broadcast domains.

- **Bridge:** A bridge connects two LANs or two segments of the same LAN and filters and forwards packets based on physical Media Access Control (MAC) addresses. A MAC address is simply a 12-alphanumeric attribute that is used to identify individual devices on the network. Using this method, a bridge can connect different network segments and manage data flow between segments. Operating at the OSI model's Data Link layer (Layer 2), a bridge reduces collisions and reduces network traffic with minor segmentation. However, it does not filter broadcasts and is expensive compared to repeaters.

- **Gateway:** A gateway connects two dissimilar networks and acts as a messenger agent, taking data from one network, interpreting it, and transferring it to another.

It also allows an organization to broaden the network, manage traffic issues, and effectively permit linking two different networks. Gateways operate at every layer; they do not filter data and are costly and difficult to manage. Protocol conversion also results in slower network performance.

- **Modem:** A modem enables a computer to transmit and receive data over telephone lines. It converts digital data to an analog audio signal and sends it over a phone line. Once the analog signal is received, the modem converts it back to a digital signal. A modem operates on either Layer 1 or Layer 2 of the OSI Model, depending on the type. A modem serves as a bridge between the LAN and the internet.

- **Repeater:** A repeater boosts the strength of a signal so that it can travel longer distances without losing quality. It is commonly used in networks to help data reach further destinations as required and where a single wireless router cannot reach all areas. A repeater operates at Layer 1 of the OSI Model, is simple to set up and inexpensive, and can connect signals with distinct types of cables. However, repeaters are unable to connect disparate networks. They also cannot distinguish between actual signals and noise and, therefore, are not able to reduce network traffic.

- **Network Interface Card (NIC):** A NIC is simply a network adapter used to connect the computer to the network. It is installed on the computer and consists of a connector to connect the cable to it, thus providing an interface between the computer and the router or modem. An NIC card is a layer of two devices and operates at both the physical and data link layers of the network model.

Figure 4.2 Arrangement of Network Devices

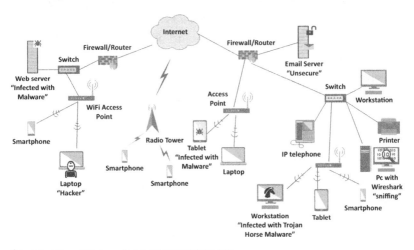

Source: https://doi.org/10.1155/2015/585432

Figure 4.2 illustrates the typical placement of network devices explained above. As shown in the figure above, each of the network devices plays its part in strengthening the cybersecurity posture of an organization. While the actual architecture can vary depending on each organization's preferences, the basic concepts remain the same. For example, a firewall is placed between the internet and the switches to protect the internal network from external cyber threats, while a router can also be incorporated to filter and forward traffic as required.

4.2 Network Security Threats

Computer networks are always at risk of attacks as they allow the attackers to effectively penetrate the whole organizational environment. The cybersecurity professional should understand the various attacks that can happen at several layers of the network and apply the relevant solutions to reduce the risks of attack. A popular tool that is often employed is the OSI reference model and its various layers. Table 4.2 shows the typical attacks per each OSI layer.

Table 4.2 OSI Model Attacks

Layer	Protocol	Attacks
Application Layer	HTTP, HTTPS, FTP, SMTP, DNS	Malware, Dos, SMTP Attack, FTP Bounce, Data Attack, Insecure HTTP, Browser Hijacking, Buffer Overflow.
Presentation Layer	Data Representation and Encryption	Malformed SSL, SSL Stripping, Unicode Vulnerabilities, Worms.
Session Layer	WEB Sockets	Session Hijacking, Dos
Transport Layer	TCP, UDP, SSL	TCP Flood, Desynchronization flooding, TCP Sequence Prediction Attack
Network Layer	IP, ICMP	Spoofing, Hijacking, Ping Floods, MITM (Man in the Middle attacks)
Data Link Layer	MAC, Ethernet	MAC Spoofing, Collision, switch looping, traffic analysis
Physical Layer	Cables, WiFi	Wire Tapping, Jamming, Tampering

Source: https://www.dickerdata.com.au

According to Table 4.2, the upper layers are more pronounced by attacks such as Denial-of-service (DoS) attacks, browser hijacking, and buffer overflow attacks as users interact with applications. In a network of DoSs, attackers flood networks with a large volume of traffic or requests, causing network resources to become overwhelmed and unavailable to legitimate users. This disrupts network operations, degrades performance, and can result in downtime for critical services.

Adversary in the Middle (AitM) and session hijacking attacks are more pronounced in the middle layers of the OSI Model. The attacker can trick a user into inputting credentials and steal sensitive information given in full trust. The lower layers are more characterized by network spoofing, in which malicious parties set up fake access points that look like legitimate networks that users can connect to. Such traps are set up in high-traffic areas frequented by employees using their mobile devices to connect to work-related applications or systems. The objective of the attacker is to access credentials and personal data. The physical layer is often affected by environmental threats such as floods, physical sabotage, and wiretapping.

4.3 Network Security Technologies

There are various types of network security technologies that you can procure and deploy to enhance your network security. Each of these has its own advantages and disadvantages, as well as implementation requirements. The following are the common network security technologies you can deploy:

A. Firewall

A firewall operates at various OSI Model layers, protecting networks from unauthorized access or malicious attacks. It enforces rules to control packet flow and acts as a sentinel, monitoring and controlling all incoming and outgoing network traffic to ensure that only authorized traffic is allowed to pass through as shown in Figure 4.3 below.

Figure 4.3 — Firewall

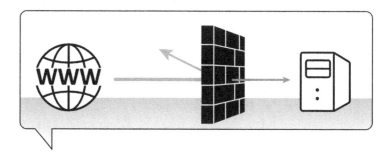

Source: https://www.itmonteur.net

A firewall can also segment networks, creating demilitarized zones (DMZs) in the process. This reduces the network's attack surface, thereby improving its security.

Table 4.3 — Types of Firewalls

Firewall Type	Description
Packet filtering firewall	This type of firewall acts as a network layer checkpoint, analyzing data packets by IP address, packet type, port number, or network protocol. It provides basic firewall functionalities, comparing incoming and outgoing packets against a standard set of predefined rules that allow or block access. They operate on Layer 3 and Layer 4 of the OSI model. They provide speed since most of the work takes place at Layer 3 or below and cannot scrutinize application-level data. They are also easily circumvented by attackers who spoof network IP addresses.

Firewall Type	Description
Stateful inspection firewall	These analyses' data at network and transport layers, inspecting the following four parameters: • The source address • The source port • The destination address • The destination port They use dynamic memory to store state tables of the incoming and established connections and offer enhanced security across all network levels, which is crucial for connectionless protocols like UDP and ICMP. However, this makes the architecture more complex, slowing operating speeds.
Proxy firewall	Proxy firewalls mask the identities of both entities. This makes it possible for each party to recognize only the proxy, thus providing robust protection between public and private networks. However, the trade-off for this high-level security is speed and cost. This is because of the extensive data processing at the application level.
Next-Generation Firewall (NGFW)	An NGFW consists of the functionalities of all the above types of firewalls and other features such as packet filtering, Port Address Translation (PAT), URL-blocking, Deep Packet Inspection (DPI), and reputation-based malware detection. INGFWs can also incorporate AI to combat sophisticated threats and block malware before it even enters the organization's technological introductory.
Web Application Firewall (WAF)	A WAF allows or blocks traffic based on predefined criteria. Web applications commonly have security vulnerabilities that can compromise a company's network and leak data. WAFs shield web applications by implementing specific rules.[22]

---

[22]. Mann, Terry. "The Most Common Types of Network Devices." Lepide Blog: A Guide to IT Security, Compliance and IT Operations, July 11, 2022. https://www.lepide.com

B. Intrusion Detection System (IDS)

An Intrusion Detection System (IDS) monitors network traffic to identify potential threats, such as exploitation attempts or imminent incidents that may compromise the network. The primary forms of IDSs are:

- **Host-based Intrusion Detection Systems (HIDS):** Host-based IDS monitors specific hosts to detect and respond to suspicious activities and attacks. As they operate strictly at the host level, they are ineffective against network threats.

- **Network-based Intrusion Detection Systems (NIDS):** A network-based IDS provides an additional layer of security by analyzing traffic for signs of potential threats. By continuously monitoring network traffic, NIDS can identify suspicious patterns or signatures that show unauthorized or malicious activity and alert system administrators or other security tools in real time.

C. Intrusion Prevention System (IPS)

An Intrusion Prevention System (IPS) identifies and blocks potential threats in real time. Once a threat is identified, the IPS takes immediate action, including dropping malicious packets, blocking traffic, or alerting administrators to prevent potential breaches or attacks on the network as depicted in Figure 4.4. below.

Figure 4.4 Intrusion Prevention Systems

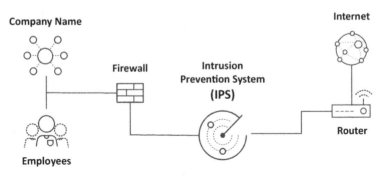

Source: https://www.paloaltonetworks.com

Types of IPS solutions include:

- **Signature-based:** This type of IPS identifies malicious activity by examining specific patterns or known malicious instruction sequences in malware.

- **Anomaly-based:** An anomaly-based IPS sets a baseline of normal behaviors of network traffic. All traffic that deviates from the baseline is blocked.

- **Heuristic-based:** This employs algorithms to analyze the traffic's behavior and is useful in preventing unknown threats or new variants of known threats.

- **Sandboxing:** Sandboxing quarantines suspicious files or payloads in a safe environment to observe their behavior without risking the broader network operations.

D. Virtual Private Network (VPN) Appliances

A VPN appliance leverages VPN technology to ensure secure, remote access to a private network. Typically, at the perimeter of the network, it enables allowed users to securely connect to internal servers and resources from anywhere outside the network, maintaining a secure and private connection.

E. Unified Threat Management (UTM)

A UTM integrates multiple security functions into a single hardware or software solution that is easily manageable. If multiple products come from different suppliers, managing a quickly unfolding network threat can be challenging. UTMs combine a network firewall, IDS, IPS, DPI, content filtering, and other features. This facilitates easier management, reporting, and maintenance. However, it should be noted that UTMs are not always better than discrete equipment, as they create a single point of failure that can take down the entire network if something goes wrong. It also leads to vendor lock-in and committing all security solutions to a sole supplier.

4.4 Wireless and Mobile Security

In today's digital landscape, securing wireless and mobile networks is of paramount importance because of the ever-evolving threat landscape and the increasing sophistication of cyber-attacks.

4.4.1 Wireless Access Points (WAPs)

A wireless access point (WAP) provides a dedicated connection point between WLANs and a wired Ethernet LAN. A service set identifier (SSID) name is required to connect to a wireless network. It identifies all systems belonging to the same network. Clients must be configured with the SSID to be authenticated to the WAP. Additionally, for security reasons, APs should be configured not to broadcast the SSID. Wireless devices come with default SSIDs, security settings, channels, passwords, and usernames, and it is advisable to change these default settings as soon as possible.

4.4.2 Threats to Wireless Networks

Understanding wireless security threats is essential to a cybersecurity professional for effectively mitigating risks and safeguarding against potential security breaches. Below are some threats to wireless networks:

- **Rogue Access Points (APs):** Rogue APs are unauthorized APs deployed without the knowledge or consent of the network administrator. Attackers can set them up to mimic legitimate APs. They can trick unsuspecting users into connecting to them, and once connected, they can intercept sensitive information and launch diverse types of attacks.

- **Evil twin attacks:** These attacks involve the creation of a malicious wireless network that impersonates a legitimate AP. The attacker then broadcasts fake SSIDs that match the names of trusted networks, thus luring unsuspecting users. Once connected, attackers can perform several types of attacks.

- **Key Reinstallation Attack (KRACK):** KRACK is a vulnerability that affects the WPA2 encryption protocol. It allows attackers to intercept and manipulate data transmitted between a client device and WAP. They can then decrypt and tamper with encrypted data, potentially compromising the confidentiality and integrity of sensitive organizational information.

- **Internet of Things (IoT) device vulnerabilities:** The proliferation of IoT devices also means an increase in vulnerabilities. This is because IoT devices lack robust security features and are vulnerable to exploitation by attackers. Malicious actors can target vulnerable IoT devices to gain unauthorized access to the network and perform several attacks on the victim.
- **Industrial Control Systems (ICS) vulnerabilities:** ICSs such as Supervisory Control And Data Acquisition (SCADA) systems are also subject to security vulnerabilities thus affecting the proper functioning of industrial processes. Some of these vulnerabilities include legal systems, outdated protocols and lack of proper segmentation thus increasing the likelihood of exposure.
- **War driving:** The broadcast range of a WAP makes internet connections available outside the organization. Attackers can drive through cities and neighborhoods with a wireless-equipped computer searching for unsecured wireless networks, an attack method known as "war driving."
- **Wireless sniffing:** This is mainly caused by connecting to unprotected public networks, which places the organization's sensitive communications or transactions at risk.[23] Because the organization connection is being transmitted "in the clear," malicious actors could use sniffing tools to get sensitive information.
- **Theft of mobile devices:** Attackers can also physically steal the organization's devices thus getting unrestricted access to all of its data, credentials, and connected cloud accounts. The data obtained can be used to perform further attacks against the victim organization. The protection methods can also be extended to individual

---

23. "Securing Wireless Networks | CISA," February 1, 2021. https://www.cisa.gov

applications and data. This is referred to as Mobile Application Management (MAM).

- **Malicious applications and websites:** Downloading a malicious application or visiting a malicious website may lead to the organization's device getting infected with malware or prompt the organization to allow a malware installation.

- **Data leakage:** Physical leakage can happen through the sharing or theft of portable storage devices, such as USB drives or external hard drives. Electronic leakage occurs when data transmission pathways are compromised by an unauthorized device, and data is stolen while in transit.

- **Mobile ransomware:** This involves the malicious actor holding the organization's device for ransom, requiring the organization to pay money or information to unlock either the device, certain features, or specific data. The organization can protect against mobile ransomware by undertaking frequent backups and updates.

- **Spyware:** Spyware is malware installed on a device without the user's knowledge or consent to gather data about the user. This information can be used to perform cyber crimes or sent to a third party thereby infringing on the user's privacy.

4.4.3 Best Practices for Securing Wireless Networks

Organizations can strengthen the security posture of their wireless networks and minimize the risk of wireless threats and attacks through the implementation of the following best practices:

- **Implement strong encryption:** Strong encryption protocols to protect data transmitted over the network by scrambling so that only allowed parties with the encryption key can decipher it. The use of encryption protocols such as Wi-Fi Protected Access 3 (WPA3) is essential for ensuring the confidentiality and integrity of data. WPA3 is the latest encryption protocol for Wi-Fi networks and offers enhanced security features such as individualized data encryption and protection against brute-force attacks.

- **Implement Multi-Factor Authentication (MFA):** MFA requires users to provide multiple forms of authentication before granting access to the network. By requiring multiple factors for authentication, MFA helps to reduce the risk of unauthorized access and strengthen the overall security posture, even if one factor is compromised.

- **Implement Certificate-Based Authentication (CBA):** CBA uses digital certificates to authenticate users and devices on the wireless network. Each device is issued a unique digital certificate, for verifying the identity of the device when connecting to the network. The method improves security as it makes it difficult for attackers to spoof or intercept digital certificates.

- **Regularly update software:** Keeping firmware and software up to date is crucial for maintaining and improving the security of wireless networks. Suppliers regularly release updates and patches to address security vulnerabilities and improve the overall stability and performance of networking devices. Organizations should implement these on a timely basis.

- **Securely configure APs:** As APs represent the gateway for devices to connect to a wireless network, they are targeted by attackers.[24] They, therefore, require greater protection. The organization should implement proper

---

24. "Re: Understanding Rogue SSID and Blocking," March 29, 2023. https://community.meraki.com

configuration settings to prevent unauthorized access and mitigate potential wireless threats.

- **Harden the network:** The organization should disable unused and unnecessary services or features to reduce the attack surface and minimize potential vulnerabilities in wireless networks. Such services include Telnet, SSH, and HTTP, which often come with the procurement of network services.
- **Change default passwords and SSIDs:** Default passwords and SSIDs are a target of attackers as they are easy to guess or exploit. These should be changed to strong passwords to prevent unauthorized access and strengthen the security of the wireless network.
- **Establish guest network:** The organization should establish the guest network functionality to allow visitors or temporary users to access the internet without compromising the security of the main wireless network.[25] This segregation reduces the risk of unauthorized access to sensitive resources or data by unauthorized personnel.
- **Deploy a VPN:** A VPN encrypts all traffic between a device and the VPN server, making it more difficult for someone to access the data in its plain form. A VPN is crucial for public Wi-Fi networks, as they are often less secure than private ones. Employees should also be aware of the importance of using a VPN when working remotely.

---

25. "Securing Wireless Networks: Practices and Emerging Threats," March 6, 2024. https://fpgainsights.com

4.5 Network Monitoring

Monitoring network traffic and activity is essential for detecting anomalous behavior and proactively responding to potential security threats in real time to prevent security incidents and attacks. The following solutions can be adopted in the monitoring of networks:

- **Network Access Control (NAC):** NAC manages device access to network resources and guarantees that only devices and users adhere to the organization's security policies. Before granting network access, NAC examines the device's security configurations against a predefined policy. Only devices meeting these criteria are permitted, while the rest are quarantined or redirected to a guest network.

- **Email security gateways:** Email gateways monitor incoming and outgoing email traffic for spam, viruses, phishing attempts, and compromised accounts. They can leverage historical data and statistical analysis to detect anomalies with more accuracy. Some suppliers sell hardware email security gateways, while others provide services alongside cloud-based email hosting. In addition, you can also strengthen security by incorporating secure email protocols such as DomainKeys Identified Mail (DKIM) and Domain-based Message Authentication, Reporting and Conformance (DMARC). DKIM adds security by adding digital signatures for verification purposes while DMARC addresses the secure handling of emails that fail DKIM checks.

- **VPN gateways:** The organization can also implement a VPN solution to provide secure access to its networks and resources. The organization may implement this solution by ensuring the host accesses the database as the VPN client software is installed before permitted access.

- **Network traffic analysis tools:** Network traffic analysis tools provide visibility into the organizations' data flows. This allows the organization's network administrators to identify potential security vulnerabilities and performance issues. This permits an organization to mitigate security threats before they become major incidents, which is less costly.

- **Proxy server:** Forward proxies retrieve data on behalf of the clients, and responses from the proxy server are returned as if coming from the original server. Proxy servers are crucial for traffic filtering and improving an organization's network performance.[26]

- **Web filter:** Web filters prevent browsers from loading pages of websites that are considered harmful or may pose security threats to an organization. The filtering is based on the URL against specified websites or web-based applications according to the filtering settings applied. Organizations should, therefore, implement web filter appliances on-premises to filter malicious Internet website content.

- **Endpoint protection:** Endpoint protection detects, quarantines, and removes various forms of malicious software at the host level. Endpoint protection may incorporate web filtering, local firewall protection, and behaviors that look for any unusual behavior of files or processes. You can also combine endpoint protection with detection to come with what is referred to as

---

26. "Network Security Devices You Need to Know About." Accessed October 3, 2024. https://blog.netwrix.com

Endpoint Detection and Response (EDR) capabilities resulting in a holistic security posture.

- **Security Event and Information Management (SIEM):** It is also crucial to implement an SIEM such as Microsoft Sentinel or Splunk for enhanced network monitoring. An SIEM system takes from security data sources such as firewalls, IDS/IPS, and endpoints for a central point for correlation and analysis. This helps in detecting correlated threats through mapping. SIEM uses cases to the MITRE ATT&CK framework, thus enabling security teams to prioritize their response efforts.

- **Zero Trust Network Access (ZTNA):** The zero trust security model states that no user should be trusted to access the organizations. It forces an organization to perform security due diligence before allowing access to the database, as only verified entities are allowed access. Being a new concept in information security, ZTNA is often confused with other terms, such as POLP. The cybersecurity professional should ensure the organization implementing the ZTNA concept is aware of what it means, and that the actual implementation is in line with the definition of ZTNA.

Chapter Summary

- Network security is the protection of data and information across networks against threats.
- The OSI Model is an important resource that cybersecurity professionals can use in the study of network security.
- An organization can deploy various types of network devices and technologies to enhance its network security infrastructure.
- A firewall is a network technology that is used to either allow or block network traffic as well as segmenting networks.
- Wireless APs are vulnerable to cyber-attacks and should be secured to enhance the overall security posture of wireless networks.
- To reduce the costs of implementing a wide range of security technologies, an organization can implement a Unified Threat Management (UTM) solution that integrates various security solutions.
- Only strong encryption in the form of WPA3 or higher should be implemented to enhance wireless security.
- The ZTNA, based on the principle of the 'never trust, always verify' principle, should be the de facto standard for protecting networks alongside the POLP.

Quiz

1. As a cybersecurity professional, you have been asked to advise between a router and a switch. What is the function of a switch?
   a. Attenuate signals
   b. Perform routine activities.
   c. Carry our filtering and forwarding of data packets.
   d. Connect dissimilar networks.

2. Network devices can be identified by the layer of the OSI Model at which they operate. Which of the following network devices operates at Layer 2?
   a. Proxy
   b. Firewall
   c. Repeater
   d. Hub

3. You have discovered that your organization's network has experienced occasional attenuation. Which device would you use to address this problem?
   a. Firewall
   b. Repeater
   c. Gateway
   d. Router

4. The proper management of sessions is crucial to network management and performance. The _____ layer establishes, manages, and ends network sessions.
   a. Application
   b. Physical
   c. Session
   d. Presentation

5. To reduce the prevalence of attacks against wireless networks, it is important for an organization to implement strong encryption. Which of the following is strong and, therefore, the most secure of the wireless security protocols?
   a. WEP3
   b. WPA3
   c. WPA2
   d. WPA

6. Your organization is considering connecting its online systems to allow for online transactions. Which of the following firewalls protects this arrangement?
   a. Packet filtering firewall
   b. Proxy firewall
   c. Stateful firewall
   d. Next-generation firewall (NGFW)

7. An intrusion prevention system (IPS) differs from an intrusion detection system (IDS) because it:
   a. Performs penetration tests
   b. Prevents attacks
   c. detects attacks only
   d. Is host-based

8. Which of the following represents a form of a passive cyberattack on the organization's network infrastructure?
   a. Scripting
   b. Traffic analysis
   c. Spoofing
   d. Distributed denial of service

9. Which of the following is a security technology that should be part of a virtual private network (VPN) technology implementation?
   a. SSL
   b. HTTP
   c. TLS
   d. FTP.

10. The cybersecurity professional should understand the differences between Wireless Equivalent Privacy (WEP) and Wi-Fi Protected Access (WPA). Which of the following represents a feature of WPA?
    a. Digital signatures
    b. Dynamic session keys
    c. Shared keys
    d. Static keys

Answers

1 – c	2 – d	3 – b	4 – c	5 – b
6 – d	7 – b	8 – b	9 – c	10 – b

CHAPTER 5
Database Security

Key Learning Objectives

- Security measures that you can implement to enhance database security
- The importance of database security in enhancing the overall cybersecurity setup of an organization
- Types of databases you can implement within your organization to enhance security
- The ACID principles and their significance in database security
- Challenges you can encounter in implementing database security solutions and strategies to overcome them

Database security is a combination of processes, tools, techniques, and controls that you use to secure and protect databases from cyber-attacks.[27] Such attacks are usually both accidental and intentional and come from both insiders and external parties.

---
27. Database Security Best Practices and Solutions | Microsoft Azure." Accessed October 18, 2024. https://azure.microsoft.com

5.1 Types of Database Models

The enormous amount of data that users consume daily shows the crucial importance of data in cybersecurity. By the end of 2024, experts projected that data creation peaked at 147 Zettabytes (ZB), from 64.2 ZB in 2020.[28] All this data has to be kept somewhere, hence the need for databases. A database model is a representation of a logical structure of the database.[29] Its purpose is to determine how data can be stored, organized in the database, and manipulated by the Database Management System (DBMS). The various database models include the following:

- Hierarchical database model
- Relational model
- Network model
- Object-oriented database mode

Let us explore these in further detail.

5.1.1 Hierarchical Database Model

The hierarchical database follows the progression of the data at certain levels, with the data categorized according to common linkage points. This results in a tree-like structure with each record related to a single parent or root, and child records are sorted in a particular order, which will be used as the physical order of the database. Figure 5.1 shows a hierarchical database.

---

[28]. "Breaking Down The Numbers: How Much Data Does The World Create Daily in 2024? | Edge Delta." Accessed October 31, 2024. https://edgedelta.com

[29]. "Database Models in DBMS: Comprehensive Guide to Relational, Hierarchical, and More." Accessed October 18, 2024. https://www.sprinkledata.com

Figure 5.1 Hierarchical Database Model

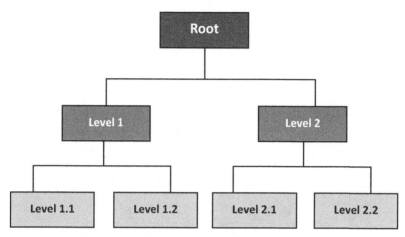

Source: https://www.javatpoint.com/types-of-databases

The hierarchical model is useful for describing many real-world relationships, as it allows data to be stored in multiple entities. The model provides quick data access in the database, therefore enhancing user productivity. However, the model is suited for linear data storage mediums, such as tapes, which are now outdated, and searching for data items is slow as the DBMS has to navigate the entire model from top to bottom to reach its destination. The model does not support many-to-many relationships and is not easily scalable.

5.1.2 Network Database Model

The network database model allows for many-to-many relationships between linked records. This results in the existence of multiple parent records in the databases, forming a network-like structure. The model is based on mathematical set theory and is constructed with multiple sets of related records, thus conveying complex relationships. Figure 5.2 depicts the network database model.

Figure 5.2 Network Database Model

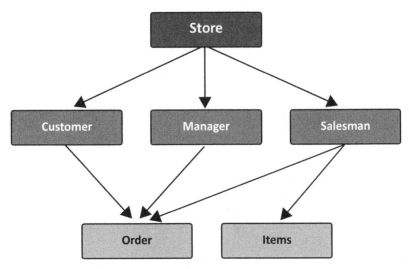

Source: https://crm.org/news/types-of-databases

The network model is simple to set up and implement and can handle one-to-many and many-to-many relationships effectively. This is very crucial in the simulation of real-world scenarios. The model can also isolate programs from complex physical storage details. However, the database structure becomes complex because of the use of pointers to maintain records, which makes it difficult to change the database structure.

5.1.3 Relational Database Model

The relational database model is one of the most popular databases in the marketplace, with data arranged as a table with columns. The cybersecurity professional should be familiar with the key terms used in relational databases, as shown in Table 5.1. Figure 5.3 shows the relational database model.

Table 5.1 Relational Model Terms

Term	Description
Relation	Table
Tuple	Row in a relation
Attribute	Characteristic defining all items in a column
Domain	Set of values that the attributes can take
Cardinality	Number of tuples in a relation
Degree	Number of attributes in relation
Primary key	Identifier that makes a table unique and can contain no null values

Figure 5.3 Relational Database Model

Table

ID	Product Name	Weight (g)	Pack
701	Honey	500	12
702	Honey	1000	6
703	Lentils	250	4

Tuples (Rows)

Cardinality = No. of rows = 3
Degree = No. of columns = 4

Attributes (Columns)

Source: https://databasetown.com/relational-database-model-operations-constraints/

Introducing relations to organize data provides the ability to make modifications without affecting data access. This makes data adjustments easier to understand and carry out. The relational model also provides both data independence and structural independence, thus simplifying database management. The relational model is easier to maintain than other database models because it hides its implementation details from the user. This reduces the complexities associated with trying to understand the inner workings of the database. However, the relational database model lacks an object-oriented paradigm and is difficult to scale, making it suitable for small databases, as large databases are typically not designed for changes.

5.1.4 Object-Oriented Database (OODB) Model

The object-oriented database model is associated with the concepts of the object-oriented programming (OOP) paradigm. Information is stored in the database as objects that can be easily called, and references can be made, significantly reducing the database workload. Figure 5.4 below shows a logical representation of the OODB model.

Figure 5.4 The OODB Model

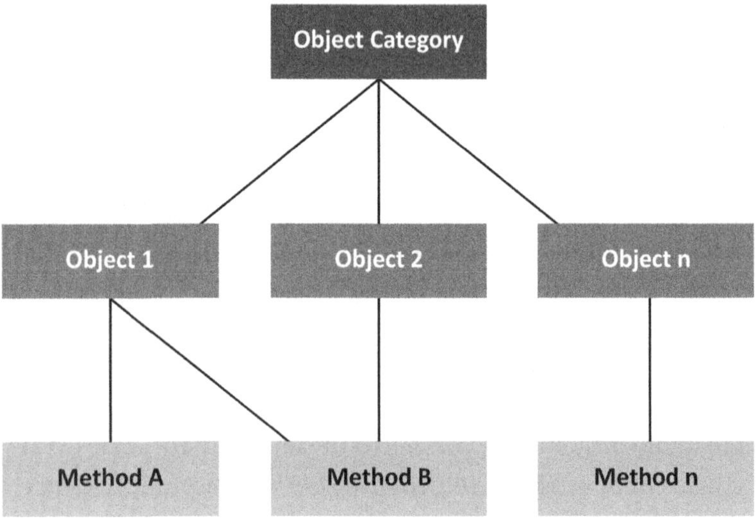

Source: https://www.ionos.ca/digitalguide/hosting/technical-matters/databases/

In Figure 5.4, different objects are linked using methods, which are simply procedures used in Object Oriented Programming. These objects comprise attributes that, in reality, represent the data elements to be defined in the database.

The OODB model provides quick and efficient responses to database queries and can support complex data structures and relationships. Through encapsulation, the model enables the reuse of tasks. It can also store various data types, including voice and video. However, the absence of a universally defined data model presents challenges in its use. OODB models are also not mature enough and still in limited use in the database marketplace, and hence still limited when compared to RDBMS usage.

5.1.5 NoSQL Databases

A NoSQL is a database model that provides a mechanism for the storage and retrieval of data and models in tabular relations that are distinct from those used in relational databases. It also comprises data structures that are more flexible than those found in relational databases.

| Figure 5.5 | NoSQL Model |

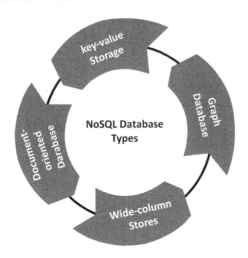

Source: https://www.prepbytes.com/blog/dbms/
types-of-databases-with-advantages-and-disadvantages

NoSQL is an open-source database and, therefore, cheap to get. It is also highly scalable and provides flexible schema, high performance, and large document sizes. The model can handle large volumes of data and is, therefore, suited for big data applications and real-time analytics. It also incorporates important features such as indexing and relationships between data. However, the NoSQL model does not provide a GUI and contains weak back-up functionalities.

5.2 Components of a Database Management System (DBMS)

A Database Management System (DBMS) can be defined as a system that allows you to manage its databases. This involves a variety of activities, including creating and updating the databases and their contents. The DBMS comprises a variety of components, each of which has a specific function that is essential to data management.[30] Table 5.2 below depicts the various components of a DBMS.

Table 5.2 Components of a DBMS

Components	Description
Hardware	This comprises all the physical devices used in a DBMS, including the computer, input/output devices, and storage devices. The hardware permitted the interaction between the software and the physical world.
Software	Software refers to all the programs and applications that are used in the database's management. This includes the DBMS software itself, the operating system, and the network software.
Data	Data is information in its raw form and is a crucial component, as without data, the database will cease to exist. Data encompasses the actual data and the metadata.
Procedures	The procedures are documented step-by-step instructions that provide useful guidance to users on how to use and manage the DBMS. They should be followed to ensure the proper functioning of the DBMS.
Data Definition Language (DDL)	The DDL refers to the language used to define the structure of the data in the database.
Data Manipulation Language (DML)	This is the language that is used to access the data, enter new data, alter data, and perform the necessary processes on the data. In using the DML, users simply enter a set of commands, and the DML will return the desired results.

---

30. LABS, [x]cube. "Understanding and Implementing ACID Properties in Databases." [x]cube LABS, March 22, 2023. https://www.xcubelabs.com

Components	Description
Data dictionary	The data dictionary is a read-only repository of information and data about the internal structure of databases in the DBMS. It is crucial to understand the meaning of the data stored in the database.
Query processor	The query processor processes all the inputs and converts them into low-level instructions before sending the output to the runtime database manager.
Run time database manager	The runtime database manager is the principal component of the DBMS that interacts with the queries sent from the database users. It manages the queries at runtime, hence the name. Its major aim is to maintain the consistency and integrity of the data in the database.
Database engine	The database engine stores, processes, and secures data in the database. It provides a controlled access mechanism to the data in the database and offers a variety of processing capabilities.
Report writer	Modern databases also comprise the report writer whose function is to extract information from different files in the dataset and present such information in the required format used in the organization.

5.3 ACID Principles

ACID is a database acronym for Atomicity, Consistency, Isolation, and Durability. Grasping these principles is critical in database security, as they allow you to define the reliability of transactions in the DBMS and attest to the security of the database and its contents. It is, therefore, a key determinant in performing database cybersecurity assessments. Table 5.3 represents a brief description of the ACID principles.

Table 5.3 Database ACID Properties

ACID Property	Description
Atomicity	Atomicity ensures all transactions are processed as a single indivisible unit and all the operations within the transaction are completed successfully or fail to process together and, therefore, are rolled back as a unit.
Consistency	Consistency requires the database to always be in a consistent state before and after in terms of all its constraints, rules, and triggers. This applies to all circumstances, including when the whole transaction fails.
Isolation	Isolation ensures each transaction is placed in isolation until its completion. This is critical in preventing data risks, such as dirty reads and non-repeatable reads, from contaminating the entire database environment.
Durability	Durability ensures that once a transaction in the dataset is committed, its changes are written and saved to the database permanently, enabling the transaction to remain intact and recoverable in case of any subsequent system failure.

ACID properties ensure the reliable and consistent processing of the database even during times of system failures, network issues, or other operations. They make the DBMS a reliable, efficient, and effective tool for handling, managing, and securing data in modern organizations. This reduces the incidence of attacks that specifically targets databases such as SQL injection and credential reuse.

However, the downside of ACID properties is that they can sometimes lead to performance overhead in the system because of the need for additional processing to ensure data consistency and integrity. They can also result in scalability issues in large, distributed dataset systems in which multiple and varying transactions occur concurrently. The ACID properties increase the complexity of the database system, which will require significant expertise and resources in terms of initial set-up and maintenance.

5.4 Database Security Risks and Controls

You should be in a position to implement controls to prevent data breaches that can pose significant risks to your organization. Some risks about data breaches you should consider include the following:

- **Data theft:** Databases are one of the prime targets for cyberattacks because they often store valuable, confidential, and sensitive information. This information includes customer records, credit card numbers, bank account numbers, and personal identification numbers, which are valuable to attackers. Malicious actors use this information to steal identities for performing unauthorized transactions and other criminal activities. For example, in 2021, a hacker stole 700 million LinkedIn data belonging to over 500 million users, which would later be sold or used to perform social engineering attacks.[31] You should note that though LinkedIn claimed no harm at the time, the incident undoubtedly exposed the users to significant risk to their data and privacy.

- **Reputational damage:** If you do not adequately protect customers' data, customers may hesitate to do business with you for fear of having their personal data disclosed. Data breaches can compromise customer information and damage the organization's reputation because of costly fines and other penalties. This may cause an overall decline in market share and overall profitability.

---

31. "LinkedIn Data Leak – What We Can Do About It - Scrubbed," July 21, 2021. https://scrubbed.net

- **Lost revenue:** A data breach can stop or slow down organizational operations and revenue generation. This may remain the case until database security challenges have been resolved and the system is fully restored. This leads to lost productivity because of inactivity during the period of data breach.

- **Increased costs:** Data breaches can cost vast sums of money in terms of the actual damage and associated costs of non-compliance, such as legal fees and regulatory fines. You may also assist victims and incur extra expenses to recover data and restore systems because of your data breaches. In extreme cases, you might also pay ransomware to cybercriminals who demand payment to restore their locked files and data, although this is illegal in most jurisdictions.

- **Fines and other penalties:** Governments (both state and federal), regulatory agencies, and standard-setting bodies may impose fines and other penalties for data breaches. They may also demand that citizens and customers be compensated when you do not protect their data. This can put a heavy strain on the organization's funds, leading to competitiveness in the marketplace. A good example is the recent case where LinkedIn Inc. was fined €310 by the Irish Data Protection Commission for processing user data without their consent.

The following are some of the security measures that you can adopt and implement to achieve and improve database security:

- **Implement firewalls:** The firewall serves as a filter to control traffic to and from the database. It blocks unwanted traffic from reaching the database while allowing network traffic to pass through. The cybersecurity professional should assess whether the firewall is properly configured with the required rules and functioning as required.

- **Deploy an Identity and Access Management (IAM) system:** Access to the database and its resources should be appropriately managed through strong identification and authentication processes. You should develop techniques to centrally manage identities and permissions to the databases to provide greater visibility and control over who accesses the database at any time. Good password management practices should also be observed and enforced always.

- **Implement authorization management:** The purpose of database authorization processes is to provide the permissions that allow you to access certain data objects. It, therefore, provides support to those dataset processes that are critical to the proper functioning of business processes. Several actions can be allowed on the database, including read, write, edit, and delete. While the database administrator assigns permissions to employees, the cybersecurity professional should ensure that this is done in a secure manner.

- **Deploy threat protection:** Auditing tracks database activities and helps maintain compliance with security standards by recording database events to an audit log. This allows you to monitor ongoing database activities, as well as analyze and investigate historical activity to identify potential threats or suspected abuse and security violations.

- **Implement data encryption:** Data encryption protects sensitive data by converting them into an alternative format so that only the intended parties can decipher them back to their original form and access them.

Although encryption does not solve access control problems, it enhances security by limiting data loss when access controls are bypassed. By strengthening data encryption, you are able to secure your data and comply with legal and regulatory requirements. You can also add data masking and tokenization to complement encryption especially in production and non-production environments respectively. Data masking replaces sensitive data with largely fake data while tokenization applies non-sensitive tokens.

- **Implement the Principle of The Least Privilege (POLP):** The POLP asserts that users and applications should have access only to the data and operations they need to perform their jobs. POLP assists you in reducing the database attack surface, thus improving the database's security posture.

- **Implement database backup data and recovery:** This is one of the critical elements to protecting information. The process involves making backup copies of the database and log files on a regular basis and storing the copies in a secure location.[32] Such backup copies should be readily available to restore the database in the event of a security breach, attack, or failure.

- **Enhance physical security:** This entails imposing strict access limits on the physical server and hardware components. With on-premises databases, you can implement robust physical security measures, including setting up physical security perimeters and using locked rooms with restricted access to the database server and other infrastructure. It's also crucial to limit access to backup media by storing it at a secure offsite location.

---

32. "Backup and Recovery of Data: The Essential Guide." Accessed October 18, 2024. https://www.veritas.com

- **Adopt the Zero Trust security model:** Database security best practices should be part of an organization's Zero Trust approach to information security. The Zero Trust motto of 'never trust, always verify' assumes breach and verifies each request as though it originates from an open database network. It validates identities and device compliance for every access request to protect people, devices, applications, and data in their various locations. The model should be deployed throughout the data lifecycle to enhance the level of protection.[33]
- **Take out cyber-insurance:** In most jurisdictions, data risks can be mitigated by taking out insurance policies to cover the same. This approach will share the risks associated with data reaches with an insurer. This frees you of the burden of proactively managing data risks, thus allowing it to concentrate on its core business.

5.5 Data Loss Prevention

Data loss prevention (DLP) refers to the various processes and procedures you can implement to prevent incidences of data loss within an organization. To enhance the effectiveness of DLP processes and interventions in an organization, various aspects should be observed, including the following:

- **Data governance:** You should ensure the existence of an effective data governance program to assist in the achievement of its data loss prevention objectives. The data governance program should consist of policies, procedures, and standards that allow you to effectively identify incidences of data loss and effectively

---

[33]. Lehr, Eliran Azulai, Brian. "Adopting a Zero Trust Approach throughout the Lifecycle of Data." Microsoft Security Blog, November 17, 2021. https://www.microsoft.com

deploy data loss prevention measures. Therefore, by implementing a resilient and effective data governance program, you become better placed to prevent data loss.

- **Data identification:** In cybersecurity, it should be noted that it is easier and less costly to prevent data loss when you have properly identified your data. This involves the identification of data, its characteristics, and its location. This calls for the development of an effective data inventory and the deployment of mechanisms meant to identify and understand the overall organizational data landscape and its sensitivity levels.

- **Data classification:** By classifying data based on certain sensitivity and risk of leaks and the impact on the organization's operations, cybersecurity teams can better prioritize DLP efforts and allocate limited resources appropriately. An effective data classification system enables you to make appropriate decisions about the data that should be accorded maximum protection against loss.

- **Data leak detection:** You should ensure that detection mechanisms for data leaks are in place before instituting preventive measures. This ensures that when preventive measures are eventually applied, they are properly configured and relevant to the organization's cybersecurity setup.

- **Data protection:** You should ensure that data is always protected throughout its lifecycle to reduce the associated impact during incidences of data loss. Security controls such as encryption and access restrictions should also be incorporated to enhance the protection of data against loss. DLP solutions should also be implemented to automatically detect and prevent suspect data leakages.

5.5.1 Types of Data Loss Threats

Data loss threats refer to any undesirable attacks that can lead to the loss of data in an organization. They include the threats shown in Table 5.4.

Table 5.4 Types of Data Loss Threats and Their Descriptions

Data Loss Threat	Description
Cyberattacks	Cyberattacks, including DDoS and SQL injection attacks, often leave loopholes through which data can be leaked. Attackers can also install malware for the sole purpose of exfiltrating organizational data. Social engineering attacks can also result in victims unintentionally losing sensitive data to attackers.
Insider threats	Insiders can also leak data, as they have trusted access to sensitive data and knowledge regarding the operating effectiveness of the data leak prevention controls in place. Hence, they have a higher likelihood of leaking data. Malicious insiders can leak information for a variety of reasons, including personal gain, retribution, or the desire to extract evidence of wrongdoing during employment termination.
	Just to show how damaging insider threats can be, a Yahoo employee allegedly downloaded 570,000 pages of source code and other proprietary information, which prompted the company to file a lawsuit against the employee.[34]

---

34. The Drum. "Yahoo Lawsuit Alleges Employee Stole Trade Secrets upon Receiving Trade Desk Job Offer." Accessed October 31, 2024. https://www.thedrum.com

Data Loss Threat	Description
Unintentional leaks	This threat occurs when employees and other organizational stakeholders unknowingly cause data loss. The cybersecurity professional should note that accidental leaks are usually simple and likely from the employees' perspective. For instance, an employee can forward sensitive information to the wrong recipients. Regular training and awareness sessions and the deployment of web filters to control what users can and cannot access help prevent data loss caused by employees.

5.5.2 Types of DLP Solutions

There are several types of DLP solutions that can be implemented, including the following:

- **Email DLP solutions:** These solutions are used to monitor email messages to identify sensitive information, block potential leaks, flag phishing frauds, and alert security teams to other potential attacks.

- **Network DLP technologies:** Network DLP technologies monitor incoming and outgoing traffic from every device connected to the network, blocking or alerting security teams to potential leaks and threats. They are deployed at the network edge to analyze traffic violating an organization's cybersecurity policies.

- **Endpoint DLP security:** These are deployed to monitor for potential leaks on laptops, servers, and mobile phones, even when these devices are not connected to the network. Endpoint-based agents can be configured to control data transfer and provide user feedback on attack attempts and actions taken.

- **Cloud DLP:** Cloud DLPs track data and IT assets being uploaded and downloaded from cloud storage and online repositories to monitor for potential leaks and misuse. To enhance effectiveness and provide comprehensive protection against data loss, you can integrate cloud DLPs with other cybersecurity technologies such as access control and encryption.

As we can see from the above discussion, data loss prevention should be a priority due to the many incidents and risks that can arise if you lose your data. A holistic approach to data protection that protects all organizational data is often recommended. You should aim to prevent data from your entire IT environment, including across networks at endpoints and in the cloud.

Chapter Summary

- Database security is the protection of data and information across networks against threats.
- The DBMS is a valuable resource that is used in the administration and management of databases.
- You can deploy diverse types of databases and database technologies to enhance data management performance depending on your particular circumstances.
- The relational model is one of the most popular databases in the marketplace today and is based on relations.
- The ACID principles are crucial in the study of databases as they show the state of transactions in the database at any given time.
- Databases are subject to several attacks, including data loss and data theft; hence, adequate and effective database controls should be implemented.
- Robust security principles such as POLP and Zero Trust should form part of the overall database security architecture.
- Data loss is the loss of organizational data intentionally or unintentionally.
- Data loss prevention is the application of processes and technologies to prevent data loss.
- DLP solutions should be deployed in such a way that they can prevent loss of data in transit, at rest, and in motion.

Quiz

1. Which of the following security measures would you implement to protect the sensitive information contained in your database?

   a. Data encryption
   b. Regular backups
   c. Database normalization
   d. Database atomicity

2. What key benefits of enhancing database security contribute to the overall cybersecurity of an organization?

   a. Reduced operational costs
   b. Prevention of unauthorized access to data
   c. Increased productivity
   d. Reduced data centralization

3. You are the cybersecurity advisor at your organization that is shopping around for a database. Which database model would you recommend if your organization seeks to store and manage large amounts of customer transaction data?

   a. Hierarchical Model
   b. Network Model
   c. Relational Model
   d. Object-Oriented Model

4. What is an understanding of the ACID principles crucial for cybersecurity purposes during transaction processing in an organization?
   a. They speed up data retrieval
   b. They ensure data integrity and consistency
   c. They reduce data storage space requirements
   d. They provide user convenience

5. There are many challenges to be tackled in implementing database security solutions in an organization. Which of the following challenges is especially critical for a healthcare database?
   a. Limited data storage
   b. Huge initial capital outlay
   c. Lack of skilled database personnel
   d. Compliance with regulatory requirements

6. In which of the following scenarios would the implementation of a hierarchical database model be MOST beneficial to an organization?
   a. Sales data analysis
   b. Employee records management
   c. Student records management
   d. Online transaction records

7. What benefit does the implementation of the network database model bring in storing data pertaining to real-world applications?
   a. Consistent data structures
   b. Simplified user navigation
   c. Efficient many-to-many relationships
   d. Reduced data redundancy

8. As a cybersecurity professional, how would you use the relational database model to manage a large dataset containing a huge amount of social media interactions?
   a. By using tree-like structures
   b. By using tables with rows and columns
   c. By linking records through pointers
   d. By encapsulating data as objects

9. Which of the following aspects allows the object-oriented database model to facilitate efficient data management, especially in software development projects?
   a. Using tuples to represent data
   b. Representing data as objects
   c. Implementing network theory
   d. Organizing data hierarchically

10. Your CISO has assigned you to procure a NoSQL database specifying that it is the best for real-time data analytics. Which of the following is a key benefit of using a NoSQL database for real-time analytics?
    a. High scalability
    b. Fixed schema
    c. Small document size
    d. Low flexibility

Answers

1 – a	2 – b	3 – c	4 – b	5 – d
6 – b	7 – c	8 – b	9 – b	10 – a

Chapter 6
Cryptography

Key Learning Objectives
- Encryption methods organizations can deploy to enhance information protection
- The various encryption mechanisms in place in the marketplace, including their pros and cons
- Hashing, its uses, and its similarities and differences with encryption
- Encryption key management and the various processes and activities involved
- The architectural setup and operations of Public Key Infrastructure (PKI)

Cryptography is a discipline of mathematics that is based on data transformation. It provides an important tool for protecting information and is used in many aspects of computer security from cyberattacks. The technology is crucial to safeguarding information whether in transit, in process, or at rest, and has become a cornerstone in modern cybersecurity.

6.1 Introduction to Encryption

Encryption transforms plain text into ciphertext, which requires the use of a unique cryptographic key for interpretation. Figure 6.1 shows the process of encryption.

Figure 6.1 Encryption Process

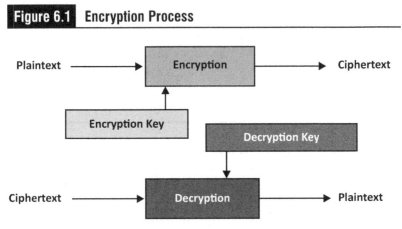

Source: https://doi.org/10.1016/B978-0-12-803843-7.00061-2

Plaintext is data that is in its original form before being subjected to encryption processes. This kind of data is intelligible to the user. Ciphertext is data that has been transformed through encryption processes. Encryption scrambles data so that they can only be read by authorized personnel, thus protecting user privacy. Attackers cannot gain access to data if they do not possess the encryption key.

6.2 Encryption Methods

Encryption methods refer to the way encryption is practiced in the real-world environment to protect information. Two types of encryption are discussed below.

6.2.1 Symmetric Encryption

Symmetrical encryption, also called private key cryptography, involves the use of a single secret key that is used to encrypt plaintext and decrypt ciphertext. It provides the following benefits:

- Simplicity and easy implementation in an organization.
- Faster performance and fewer resources required.
- Best suited to encrypt large data sets.

Disadvantages include the following:

- It is a less secure method compared to asymmetric encryption.
- The key distribution becomes complex, causing security risks. Therefore, it is less ideal for many users.
- The method is not suited to the encryption of smaller data sets.
- The strength of symmetric encryption inherently relies on key secrecy, and key compromise exposes the data to huge risks.

6.2.2 Asymmetric Encryption

Also known as public key cryptography, asymmetric encryption involves the use of two keys — a public key and a private key — for both the encryption and decryption processes, respectively. The public key is publicly available, while the corresponding private key is, as its name suggests, private. We use the public key for encryption, while the private key is used for decryption. The advantages of asymmetric encryption include the following:

- This method provides a high level of security to the data, which makes online transfers safer.

- It eliminates the burden of sharing a private key with the receiver.
- The public key is public, allowing anyone to send secured messages to the key owner.

However, asymmetric encryption suffers from the following weaknesses:

- The method is slower than symmetric encryption and hence not efficient for larger volumes of data.
- It involves extensive calculations for key generation and data transformation and slows performance speeds.

6.3 Encryption Mechanisms

An encryption algorithm, also known as a cipher, refers to the methods and instructions used to transform data into ciphertext. Figure 6.2 shows how WhatsApp encryption works in real life.

Figure 6.2 WhatsApp Encryption

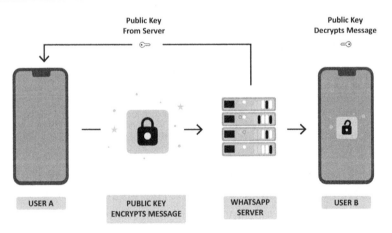

Source: https://www.wati.io/blog/understanding-whatsapp-data-security-understand-end-to-end-encryption-and-backups/

As shown in Figure 6.2, User A encrypts the message using his/her public key with User B decrypting the message using his/her private key. The whole process happens automatically without user participation. The WhatsApp application automatically generates both the private and public key pairs upon installation. The private key is kept securely while the public key is shared with other users. When you generate a message, WhatsApp automatically encrypts the message using your recipient's public key and sends the message to WhatsApp servers. The recipient device will decrypt the message using its private key, thus completing the end-to-end encryption.

You should note that the effectiveness of the overall encryption system depends on the length, functionality, and features of the encryption system in use.

Commonly used symmetric encryption algorithms include:

- **Advanced Encryption Standard (AES):** AES is a symmetrical encryption algorithm that operates on fixed block sizes of 128 bits with keys that can be 128, 192, or 256 bits long. This flexibility allows for a balance between speed and security, depending on needs. The algorithm is implemented to secure data in key institutions such as government agencies and financial institutions.

- **Data Encryption Standard (DES):** DES is a block cipher, so a cryptographic key and algorithm are applied to a block of data simultaneously rather than one bit at a time. During the encryption process, DES groups plaintext data into 64-bit blocks. Triple DES is an enhanced version of DES that encrypts data blocks using a 56-bit key and applies the DES cipher algorithm three times to each data block. Triple DES can be deployed in a variety of operating environments. For example, financial institutions can use the method to encrypt Automated Teller Machine (ATM) passwords.

- **Blowfish:** Blowfish is a symmetric block cipher that encrypts data in 64-bit blocks with a variable-length key up to 448 bits. The method is effective in encrypting data on a smaller scale. While it is a cost-effective solution as it is free to use without licensing restrictions, with a 64-bit block size, the algorithm is vulnerable to certain attacks. Twofish succeeded Blowfish and is an enhancement in terms of speed and security. It can encrypt data in 128-bit blocks and support key sizes of 128, 192, or 256 bits, thus providing a high level of security.

Common asymmetric encryption methods include:

- **Rivest Shamir Adleman (RSA):** RSA is an advanced asymmetric encryption algorithm and one of the most popular asymmetric encryption algorithms in use today. The method is based on the factorization of the product of two large prime numbers and provides secure protection due to its advanced mathematical properties and complexity. This makes it a very dependable encryption method when transmitting confidential data. However, the efficiency of RSA tends to decrease when encrypting large volumes of data.
- **Elliptic Curve Cryptography (ECC):** ECC is a public-key cryptography method that is considered stronger than RSA encryption in the marketplace. The advantage of ECC is that it uses shorter keys, which makes it faster and more efficient. The method is usually used in modern Transport Layer Security (TLS) protocols to strengthen web communications security. ECC is deployed in a variety of functional areas, including email encryption and cryptocurrencies.

- **Digital Signature Standard (DSS):** This standard uses the digital signature algorithm to allow users to perform encryption using digital signatures. To perform the encryption process using DSS, you sign the encrypted message with your private key; the recipient will use the corresponding public key to open the message. A crucial point to note regarding the DSS is that it is not a single algorithm but a suite of algorithms that work in unison to generate and validate digital signatures.

6.3.1 Stages in Data Encryption

Cybersecurity professionals should be aware of the various stages at which data is encrypted. Table 6.1 shows the stages in encryption:

Table 6.1 Stages in Data Encryption

Stage of Encryption	Description
Encryption at rest	Data at rest means files stored on hard drives, cloud storage, USB devices, and smartphones. You should ensure that data at rest is encrypted to protect against unauthorized access. It is also crucial to ensure that the encryption key is protected using secure methods such as Cloud HSM.
Encryption in Transit	Data in transit or in motion should be protected with encryption as it traverses networks. Such data is at risk of unauthorized access or interception by threat actors who have access to the same networks. Encryption in transit protects data moving over the internet using various methods such as Secure Sockets Layer (SSL), Transport Layer Security (TLS), and Secure File Transfer Protocol (SFTP).

Stage of Encryption	Description
Encryption in use	Data in use or in process is neither at rest nor in transit but is data that is being worked upon. Data in use is typically viewed, edited, or deleted. You should note that mobile and cloud applications constantly have data in use. Data in use is susceptible to threats depending on where the data lives on the system and who can access and/or use it. This means that such data should be secured using the most secure encryption methods.

6.4 Encryption Key Management

Encryption key management refers to policies and procedures for generating, distributing, storing, organizing, and protecting cryptographic keys. An encryption key management system includes the stages shown in Table 6.2. Note that the exact order of the encryption key lifecycle can change depending on the situation. Sometimes, you might skip phases entirely.

Table 6.2 Stages in Encryption Key Management

Stage	Description
Key generation	Key generation involves the use of an encryption algorithm to create a new key. If you generate a key with a weak encryption algorithm, then any attacker could easily discover the value of the encryption key. Generating keys in insecure locations is not advisable as it increases the risk of compromise.

Stage	Description
Key storage	You need to store the key for safety and easy access somewhere far away from the data it seeks to protect. It is best to keep operational keys in an encrypted environment for added security. The key must be stored safely for later decryption.
Key distribution	Once a key is ready to use, it must be securely transferred. A key management system facilitates this process, ensuring that only allowed entities can access the key. The most secure way is to distribute the keys using secure Transport Layer Security (TLS) connections. This assists in the maintenance of the security of the keys under distribution. Using an insecure connection to distribute the cryptographic keys can result in threat actors successfully executing attacks along the network.
Key usage	This is the stage when the keys are active and operational and used for cryptographic operations. You should ensure that the keys are limited to only one purpose, as using the same key for two different cryptographic processes can weaken security. Once a key is ready to use, ensure its secure transfer. A key management system facilitates this process, ensuring that only authorized entities can access the key.
Key rotation	During key rotation, you simply replace the older keys with new ones. It is crucial to regularly rotate keys to maintain security because the longer the key is in use the greater the chances of compromise. Key rotation can happen before expiration, especially when there are suspicions that the key may have been compromised.

Stage	Description
Key Revocation	Keys that are no longer needed or are compromised should be disabled and promptly deleted. This prevents unauthorized access to sensitive data and eliminates the risk of old and outdated keys falling into the wrong hands. Removing a key means that the key can no longer be used to encrypt or decrypt data, even if its operational period is still valid.
Key destruction	When you destroy a key, it is permanently removed from any key manager database or other storage method. It is difficult or impossible to recreate the key unless you use a backup key. Deactivated keys can also be kept in an archive to allow for reconstruction of the keys if data encrypted in the past must now be decrypted by that key or key pair.

6.4.1 Key Management Risks

Various threats can compromise keys; hence the need for effective key management in an organization. The challenge with these threats is that you may not detect a key compromise until the attacker uses it. The following are some of the key management risks that organizations face:

- **Weak keys:** The key should be generated using a certified random number generator and be of sufficient length to further enhance strength. You should, however, ensure that the strength of the key is commensurate with the value of the data it is protecting and the time for which it needs to be protected.

- **Incorrect use of keys:** Each key should be generated for a single, specific purpose in an organization. This means you can generate a key specifically for an intended security objective, such as protecting an application. If you use the key for some other purpose that was not originally intended, it may not offer a sufficient level of security.

- **Reuse of keys:** Improper reuse of keys in certain circumstances can make it easier for an attacker to crack the key. This should be avoided in an organization. Ideally, every key should be used for a single purpose and subsequently retired or destroyed.
- **Non-rotation of keys:** If a key is overused, then it makes the key more vulnerable to cracking, especially when using older symmetric algorithms; it also means that a high volume of data is exposed in the event of key compromise. To avoid this, you should rotate keys at appropriate intervals.
- **Inappropriate key storage:** You should avoid storing the keys along with the data they protect. This increases the risks of unauthorized access as any exfiltration of the protected data is also likely to compromise the key as well.
- **Inadequate protection of keys:** Using manual key management processes, paper, or inappropriate tools such as spreadsheets accompanied by manual key ceremonies can easily result in human errors. The major risk is that human errors often remain undetected, rendering the keys highly vulnerable.

6.4.2 Mitigating Key Management Risks

A variety of methods can be used to mitigate the risks associated with key management in an organisation, including the following:

- **Automate key management:** The use of electronic key management systems is one of the most effective ways to mitigate key management risks. It involves the use of a dedicated Hardware Security Module (HSM), a physical device that is used to securely generate, store, and manage encryption keys. HSMs can also be stored in the cloud and provide tamper-resistant protection.

- **Limit key access:** You can limit key access using the POLP, allowing you to identify potential key incidents and revoke affected keys promptly. The POLP ensures that only authorized users can access important cryptographic keys while providing better tracking of key usage. It also limits the effects of a compromised key to only a few people with access to the key.

- **Avoid hard-coding keys:** The most important practice with cryptographic keys is never to use hard-coded key values anywhere. Hard-coding a key is risky as it compromises the key use and allows unauthorized access to the encryption key values. This risk also increases when the keys are hard-coded into open source allowing anyone access to the code.

- **Segregate duties:** Separating duties related to key management is another important practice. One person should be assigned to authorize new user access to keys, another distributes the keys, and a third person creates the keys. With this method, the first person cannot steal the key during the distribution or learn the value of the key during the generation phase of the key lifecycle.

- **Split keys:** To ensure the strength of any key management system, we split the keys into multiple portions. The idea behind split keys is that no single person should know the full key; rather, multiple people must collaborate to use the key. This ensures that others can be held accountable by their peers if their part of the key is compromised.

6.5 Hashing

Hashing is the process that uses mathematics to generate a fixed-size output from an input of variable size.[35] The mathematical formulas used are known as hash functions, while the fixed-length, unique outputs are known as hash values, or simply, a hash. The method is applied in a variety of functions, such as password storage, data integrity checks, and digital signatures. Figure 6.3 shows how the hashing process works.

Figure 6.3 How Hashing Works

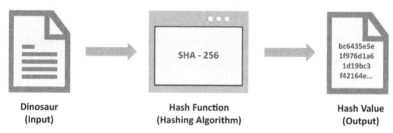

| Dinosaur | Hash Function | Hash Value |
| (Input) | (Hashing Algorithm) | (Output) |

Source: https://codesigningstore.com/what-is-hashing-algorithm-how-it-works

- **Input data is key:** The user determines what should be hashed in the form of input data (also known as the hash key). A key can be in any format: a string of text, a list of numbers, or an image.
- **The hash function:** The hash function is the key part in the whole hashing process as it deals with the actual conversion of key inputs into characters of fixed-length strings. It transforms the message into a predetermined bit size consisting of a series of equal-sized blocks that are compressed in sequence.

---

35. GeeksforGeeks. "Introduction to Hashing," July 4, 2022. https://www.geeksforgeeks.org

- **The hash value:** The hash value is the final output of passing data through a hash function. This value should be unique to each input and can only be used once for data protection or any other purposes. If hash values are not immediately needed, they can be securely stored in hash tables.

6.5.1 Characteristics of Hashing

The following are some of the important characteristics that you should be aware of in the application of hashing:

- **One way:** Hashing is 'one-way' in nature, and the operations associated with it are irreversible. This means that you can easily convert input data into a hash, but you cannot retrieve the original data. This is a marked difference from encryption, where the data can be converted to plaintext.

- **Deterministic:** The deterministic nature of hashing means that if two different users input the same data using the same hashing algorithm, the resultant hash value should be similar.[36] This helps in ensuring consistency in the protection of data.

- **Mathematical:** Hashing relies on strict rules that underlie the work a hashing algorithm performs. These rules are pre-determined and rigid and cannot be altered. The complexity of the message digest is tied to the complexity of the associated mathematical computations.

- **Uniform:** The user can only select a single type of hashing algorithm at any given time. Any data subjected to hashing processes will produce a fixed output. It is

---

36. Team, Codecademy. "What Is Hashing, and How Does It Work?" Codecademy Blog (blog), April 28, 2023. https://www.codecademy.com

also important to note that the hashing algorithm only performs one action, that is, compressing data and nothing else.

6.5.2 Differences Between Encryption and Hashing

You may have realised that encryption and hashing are largely similar, and it is easy to confuse these two cybersecurity concepts. However, the terms are different and should not be used interchangeably. Table 6.3 shows the main differences.

Table 6.3   Encryption vs Hashing

Characteristic	Encryption	Hashing
Objective	To ensure message confidentiality	To ensure message integrity
Direction	Two-way and reversible	One-way and irreversible
Key requirements	Encryption keys are required	No encryption keys are required
Output	Output is variable	Strictly fixed length

6.5.3 Application of Hashing

You can apply hashing in a variety of situations, including the following:

- **Blockchain:** This is one of the most known applications of hashing and is associated with cryptocurrencies such as Bitcoin. Every record or transaction is known as a block and includes the transfer amount, the timestamp, and the hash value for the data from the previous block. This means that any attempts to modify the transaction history will cause the hash values and will be immediately detected.

- **Password storage:** As part of its security measures, an organization must keep records of its identities that all the members use to access its resources. However, if these identities are not securely stored, threat actors may find an entry and compromise the identities. The application of hashing in this scenario ensures that the passwords cannot be tampered with.

- **Digital signatures:** Hashing is also applied in digital signatures to ensure non-repudiation of messages by the sender. Signing the message digest makes it difficult for the sender to deny accountability. Hashing ensures that even a small change in the data is detected, thereby ensuring the integrity of the digital signature.

- **Document management:** Hashing algorithms can authenticate the data where the document author can apply a hash to a document to ensure the integrity of the contents. This hash forms a seal of approval, and if the recipient compares it with the original upon receipt and the documents match, it follows that the document would not have been tampered with in transit.

- **File and database management:** Organizations are increasingly using hashes to index data, identify files, and delete duplicates from their databases. For example, suppose your database system consists of hundreds of files; you can save time by applying hashes for indexing purposes. This is true when you are working with large databases, and you do not need to navigate through each record.

6.5.4 Popular Hashing Algorithms

A variety of hashing algorithms have been and continue to be developed by various entities worldwide. Each of these algorithms has its methods, merits, and demerits. Table 6.4 shows some of the most popular hashing algorithms in use today.

Table 6.4 Hashing Algorithms

Hashing Algorithm	Description
Message Digest 5 (MD5):	MD5 consists of a hash size of 128 and is extensively used in storing sensitive information such as passwords and credit cards. Though very popular during its early days, repeated and frequent collisions had reduced its preference among several organizations. It is also slow, which further reduces its use in today's demanding environments.
Secure Hash Algorithm (SHA):	SHA is a collection of hashing algorithms that has grown to become the standard algorithm for hashing private data. It takes many variations: SHA-12 produces hash values comprising 64-bit values, while SHA-256 produces a 256-bit hash value and is considered more secure than MD5.
Cyclic Redundancy Check (CRC32)	This hashing algorithm is deployed when the primary purpose of hashing is simply to detect errors and changes in data. The preferable option in such cases is to perform checks using a cyclic redundancy check (CRC) code. Cybersecurity professionals can also deploy CRC32 hacking techniques to check file integrity.

6.6 Public Key Infrastructure (PKI)

Public Key Infrastructure (PKI) is a set of technologies and processes that are used to protect and authenticate digital communications. It provides a framework that seeks to protect and authenticate communications between servers and users. It can also be used for secure communications within an organization to ensure that the messages are not tampered with in transit. Figure 6.4 below graphically depicts PKI.

Figure 6.4 How PKI Works

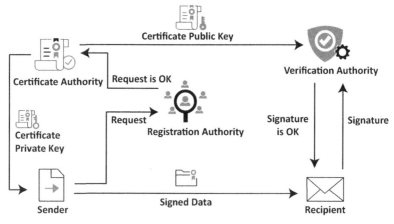

Source: https://www.researchgate.net/figure/Public-Key-Infrastructure-AppViewX-2020_fig1_351247755

As can be discerned from Figure 6.4, suppose you would like to send a secure message to your recipient. You obtain the recipient's digital certificate from a trusted Certificate Authority (CA). This certificate will contain your recipient's public key. You will use that public key to encrypt your email. Upon receipt of your email, the recipient will use the corresponding private key to decrypt your email. This ensures security in communications and can be applied in various environments that require highly secure communications, such as banks, health services, and government agencies.

6.6.1 Components of PKI

The major components of PKI are shown in Table 6.5.

Table 6.5 PKI Components

PKI Component	Description
Digital Certificate	A digital certificate, also known as an X.509 certificate, serves as an electronic identification that facilitates the verification of identities across organizations during online transactions. It offers proof of identity to a requesting entity, which is verified by a third party. The PKI certificate should comprise the following elements: • Distinguished name (DN) of the owner • Owner's public key • Date of issuance • Expiration date • DN of the issuing CA • Issuing the CA digital signature
Certificate Authority (CA)	The CA is the entity that is responsible for the management of all PKI certificates. In a PKI system, the client generates a public-private key pair and transmits the public key and information to be imprinted on the certificate to the CA. The CA then creates a digital certificate using the user's public key and certificate attributes.

PKI Component	Description
Registration Authority (RA)	The RA verifies the identity of the user or device that requests the digital certificate. This can be a third party, or the CA can also function as an RA. An important point to take note of here is that while the CA authorizes the RA to verify the certificates, the CA retains the prerogative to issue the certificates.
Certificate database	This database stores the digital certificate and its associated metadata. It also includes details as to the length of time the certificate will be valid.
Central Directory	The Central Directory represents a secure location that is dedicated to the safekeeping and indexing of cryptographic keys.
Certificate Policy (CP)	This policy outlines the PKI's operating processes and procedures. It is mainly used by external parties to determine the trustworthiness of the PKI.
Certificate Practice Statement (CPS)	The CSP is a document that details the methods and standards that the CA uses in the management of digital certificates.
Certificate Revocation List (CRL)	When a certificate is revoked, it becomes unusable for establishing secure connections, rendering it untrusted by web browsers and other client applications. Revocation of the certificate is essential to prevent potential security breaches and protect you from unknowingly connecting to websites or services that have lost trustworthiness.

6.6.2 Certificate Revocation

Certificate revocation is the invalidation of a certificate before it reaches its natural expiration date. An important point to note is that when the certificate is revoked, it becomes unusable because it is untrusted across all systems.

The CA should, therefore, immediately replace all revoked certificates to restore and maintain secure communications. The following are the main reasons why certificates are revoked:

- **Compromised private key:** This is one of the main reasons for certificate revocation in organizations. Once the private key is compromised, it should be revoked immediately before it falls into the hands of threat actors. The CA should revoke the certificate, thus rendering the use of the compromised private key ineffective.

- **Change in the certificate holder's status:** Sometimes, certificate holders change, which renders the certificate invalid. For example, an employee holding a certificate may leave the organization, rendering the certificate unreliable for continued use. The next logical step for the CA to take in such scenarios would be to revoke the certificate.

- **Fraudulent certificates:** Sometimes, certificates may be fraudulently issued due to the activities of fraudsters or mistakes and malicious activities by inside personnel. The CA should actively monitor for suspicious or unauthorized certificates, and any detection of fraud should lead to an immediate revocation of the certificate, thus maintaining the integrity of the PKI.

- **Certificate expiration:** This may not exactly fit in the definition of revocation in the traditional sense but it's equally important. Certificates should be rendered invalid if they pass their expiration date and should be rendered not fit for use. Invalid certificates should be transferred to the CRL to alert would-be users of their invalidity. This is an initiative-taking approach to maintaining a secure PKI infrastructure.

Chapter Summary

- Encryption transforms plain text data into cipher text that cannot be decrypted without the knowledge of the decryption key. This helps maintain secure communication channels inside and outside of the organization.
- Symmetric encryption involves the use of a single key, while asymmetric encryption requires two keys, one private and the other public.
- Failure to properly manage encryption keys can lead to serious security risks as the keys can fall into the hands of criminals, leading to unauthorized exposure of organizational data.
- Hashing is a technique that transforms variable data inputs into fixed-size output known as a message digest.
- The Public Key Infrastructure (PKI) leverages encryption technologies to enable secure communications across participating organizations.
- Key components making up the PKI include digital certificates, CAs, RAs, and CRLs.

Quiz

1. Which of the following methods should a financial institution implement to ensure that sensitive transaction data is only readable by authorized personnel without the complexities involved in exchanging encryption keys?
   a. Hashing
   b. Symmetric Encryption
   c. Asymmetric Encryption
   d. Data compression

2. Which method would you choose if you need to encrypt large datasets quickly and efficiently?
   a. Symmetric Encryption
   b. Asymmetric Encryption
   c. Public key encryption
   d. Hashing

3. Your organization would like to eliminate the burden of sharing a private key with its stakeholders while ensuring high security for its online transactions. Which of the following encryption methods should you adopt?
   a. Symmetric Encryption
   b. Asymmetric Encryption
   c. Hashing
   d. PKI

4. A government agency would like to employ an encryption algorithm that balances speed and security with flexible key lengths (128, 192, or 256 bits) and has approached you for advice. Which of the following algorithms would you advise them to implement?

   a. DES
   b. Blowfish
   c. AES
   d. RSA

5. Which of the following encryption methods involves grouping plaintext data into 64-bit blocks and applying the encryption algorithm three times to each block to enhance security?

   a. Triple fish
   b. DES
   c. Triple DES
   d. Twofish

6. You run a small business, and you are shopping around for a cost-effective encryption solution that does not require licensing. You also need to be able to encrypt 64-bit blocks with a variable-length key. Which of the following would you buy?

   a. AES
   b. Blowfish
   c. DES
   d. ECC

7. Which of the following encryption methods is based on the factorization of two large prime numbers?
   a. Blowfish
   b. AES
   c. RSA
   d. DSS

8. Which of the following methods involves splitting keys into multiple portions to prevent any single individual from knowing the full key?
   a. Split keys
   b. Dual control
   c. Segregation of duties
   d. Least privilege

9. Which of the following is the best approach for generating strong encryption keys?
   a. Using large prime numbers
   b. Using a random generator
   c. Using hard-coded keys
   d. Adding factorization to the process

10. A large multinational corporation has approached you for advice regarding the setting up of a comprehensive system for managing digital certificates and public-key encryption to secure its various communications. Which of the following architectural setups would you advise them to implement?

    a. Symmetric Encryption
    b. Asymmetric Encryption
    c. Zero Trust
    d. PKI

Answers

1 – b	2 – a	3 – b	4 – c	5 – c
6 – b	7 – c	8 – a	9 – b	10 – d

Case Study 2

Implementation of Encryption Strategies

Overview

Smart Technologies is a hypothetical medium-sized technology company based in the Silicon Valley Area in California in the US. The company focuses on mobile application development, employing several software developers. It develops mobile applications for a wide range of businesses in the whole of the US as well as the international markets. With the expansion of the size of the company, the management recognized the necessity of using effective encryption methods to secure confidential data and guarantee cybersecurity.

Encryption Strategy Roadmap

Smart Technologies process significant quantities of sensitive client information, which necessitates the use of encryption techniques so that an unauthorized party does not access this data. Their management also chose both symmetric and asymmetric encryption techniques to further improve their data security.

- **Symmetric Encryption:** Smart Technologies use symmetric encryption (i.e., private key cryptography) to decrypt very large datasets. This approach offered simplicity, higher performance, and thus less resource consumption. However, the company had to address the challenges of key distribution and ensure the secrecy of the encryption keys to prevent compromise.

- **Asymmetric Encryption:** To protect data during online transmissions and to bypass the responsibility of transferring a private key, Smart Technologies used asymmetric encryption (public key cryptography). This method involved using a public key for encryption and a private key for decryption. On the one hand, it offered a strong security guarantee for information, and everybody could securely transmit information to the owner of the key.

Impact

By employing symmetric and asymmetric encryption schemes, Smart Technologies has enhanced its data protection more efficiently and effectively. The application of these encryption schemes enabled the corporation to secure massive datasets effectively and to transmit them safely online. This resulted in increased client trust and satisfaction, as well as enhanced overall cybersecurity.

Discussion Questions:

1. What are the advantages and disadvantages of symmetric encryption at Smart Technologies, and how did the company solve the key distribution problem?
2. How did asymmetric encryption enhance the security of online data transfers for Smart Technologies, and what are the potential weaknesses of this method?
3. What are the key differences between symmetric and asymmetric encryption, and why did Smart Technologies decide to implement both methods?

Chapter 7
Identity and Access Management

Key Learning Objectives
- The importance of Identity and Access (IAM) and related technologies
- The reasons for identification, authentication, and authorization
- The rationale behind the implementation of Identity Governance and Administration Solutions (IGA)
- Identity as a Service (IDaaS), its use cases, and its application in modern IAM
- Implementing Privileged Identity Management (PIM) solutions and best practices
- Current IAM trends and their implications for organizational operations

Identity and Access Management (IAM) is a security arrangement that comprises policies, controls, and solutions that facilitate the management of digital identities. A digital identity is any online information about a person or entity that allows access to system resources. Cybersecurity professionals should understand an organization's IAM strategy to be in a position to properly advise the organization on the ways to enhance the security of IAM systems.

7.1 Introduction to IAM

The crucial importance of IAM in an organization is to ensure that all users can be identified and authenticated before they are allowed to access organizational systems. This helps ensure a strong security environment and prevents unauthorized access and subsequent attacks. Beyond the basic concepts of identification and authentication, IAM also comprises a variety of processes and technologies, which we will discuss in this chapter, including Identity as a Service (IDaaS), Identity and Governance Administration (IGA), and Privileged Identity Management (PIM).

7.2 Identification, Authentication, and Authorization

The above terms are often mistakenly used interchangeably; however, they are not the same and work differently to achieve specific tasks. Figure 7.1 illustrates this relationship.

Figure 7.1 Identification, Authentication, and Authorization

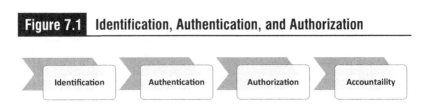

7.2.1 Identification

This is the first step in most online transactions and requires you to 'identify' yourself, usually by providing a name, email address, or phone number. Identification works the same whether in a virtual setting or a physical setting. For example, a security officer may require proof of identification before you can be allowed entry into organizational premises. In the same manner, a virtual system may require you to identify yourself with an ID, a username, or any other acceptable identifier.

7.2.2 Authentication

During authentication, you provide proof of identity for verification purposes. There are many methods used to verify identities, including the following:

- **Something you know (knowledge factor):** The most common example of this type of information would be a password. A key point to note, however, is that a password on its own is a weak form of authentication and is prone to a variety of risks, such as dictionary attacks and brute force attacks.

- **Something you have (possession factor):** This could be a unique physical item, such as a smartphone or an access card, a cryptographic key, or a fob/RSA token that receives or generates a temporary passcode.

- **Something you are (inherent factor):** Biometric authentication factors are inborn, and you can confirm your identity through an inherent physical identifier such as an iris, face, or fingerprint. Behavioral biometrics, such as typing speed, voice, or signature, can also be used.

Types of Authentication Factors

Authentication Factors can be combined in a variety of ways to strengthen security. The following are some of the major types of authentication factors:

- **Single-Factor Authentication (SFA):** This requires one authentication factor to prove your identity. Providing your username and password to log in to a social media site is a typical example of SFA.

- **Multi-Factor Authentication (MFA):** MFA requires at least two authentication factors of two diverse types, such as a password (knowledge factor) and a fingerprint scan (inherent factor). MFA can provide you with an elevated level of certainty that the person attempting access is truly who they claim to be.

- **Two-Factor Authentication (2FA):** 2FA is a specific type of MFA that requires exactly two factors. You may have experienced 2FA when your bank gives you a password option and a code sent to your phone to log into your account.

7.2.3 Authorization

Authorization is granting the user access to services or the system, thus permitting rights and privileges based on the identification and authentication already provided. It answers the question: What are you allowed to do once you are logged into the system? The authorization process protects organizational resources in a system and their users.

Consider a sensitive database containing employees' records in your organization. Authorization determines what you can do within the database. You can be authorized to view the files, update them, delete them, or perform any other function that is deemed acceptable to your level of access.

Types of Authorization

The type of authorization a user is provisioned with depends on the access level assigned. There are several levels of access control, including the ones mentioned in Table 7.1.

Table 7.1 Types of Authorization

Type of Authorization	Description
Role-Based Access Control (RBAC)	This method provisions access permissions and related entitlements based on job roles within an organization. For example, suppose you are a junior-level cybersecurity analyst, and you are allowed to view firewall configurations in an organization. This should be adequate for you, as more senior roles, such as senior cybersecurity analysts, are given full administrative access.
Attribute-Based Access Control (ABAC)	ABAC uses certain attributes, such as your name, the type of resources, and the time of day to determine access levels and, therefore, what you are authorized to do in the system. The system will analyze all relevant attributes and only grant access if certain predefined criteria are met. For example, you may be able to access sensitive data only during work hours or when you hold a certain managerial level in an organization.
Mandatory Access Control (MAC)	MAC systems are implemented where you seek to enforce centrally defined access control policies across all the users in the organization. They provide blanket control settings on a more granular level than both the RBAC and ABAC systems. Access to an organization's sensitive information assets is based on set clearance levels or trust scores.

Type of Authorization	Description
Discretionary Access Control (DAC)	DAC enables the owners of resources to set their own access control rules for those resources. The DAC method has the advantage of being more flexible than the other methods of access control described above. They allow the owners of the information assets to make decisions regarding who can access and act upon such assets.

7.3 Identity Governance and Administration (IGA)

Identity Governance and Administration (IGA) combines the practices of identity governance and identity administration activities to enable the efficient management of identities and access processes throughout an organization. It improves their visibility into identities and access privileges and helps them implement controls to prevent inappropriate or risky access:

- **Identity Governance:** This deals with governance aspects such as visibility, segregation of duties, role management, attestation, analytics, and reporting.

- **Identity Administration:** This term is related to account administration, credentials administration, provisioning, and the management of entitlements in an organization.[37]

7.3.1 The Need for IGA

Increasing digitization means more devices and data across on-premises and multi-cloud/remote environments,

---

37. "IAM's 4 Core Pillars – IGA, AM, PAM, AD Management." Accessed November 27, 2024. https://www.oneidentity.com

which requires IGA solutions to perform the following functions, among others:

- **Manage identities:** Changes in user associations within an organization (for example, due to resignations and transfers) will also lead to changes in access requirements. IGA solutions enable organizations to easily manage these changes and help maintain control over system resources.

- **Track risky access requests:** An IGA system provides a central approval location, making it easy for you to request the access approvals you need to meet your responsibilities. The centralization of access requests also enables security administrators to effectively identify and resolve security threats.

- **Improve security and compliance:** Detailed reports and analytics help IT administrators understand what is happening in your environment and find any problems or risks. This enables them to troubleshoot problems effectively to protect and audit access reports to meet compliance requirements.

- **Improve accessibility:** With robust IGA solutions, you can allow and control remote access safely to maintain business continuity while also preventing breaches. Such flexibility enables employees to work from anywhere, and thus improves their productivity and performance. Automated workflows also assist in enhancing efficiency and reducing operational costs.

7.3.2 Features of IGA Solutions

IGA solutions enable organizations to streamline their identity lifecycle management accurately and efficiently. They include the following elements:

- **Integration connectors:** Connectors enable IGA tools to integrate with directories and other systems that contain information about the organization, the applications, and systems to which they have access, and their authorization within those systems. These connectors read these data to understand who has access to what. They also write data to create a new account and grant them access.

- **Identity federation:** In identity federation, you can access multiple applications and domains using a single set of credentials. This ensures secure linkages between your identity and multiple identity management systems, allowing you to access different applications and platforms securely and efficiently. It also makes it easier to manage security risks associated with identities, permissions, and entitlements.

- **Automated workflows:** Automated workflows make it easier for you to request access to the systems they need to do their job. Moreover, administrators can easily onboard and offboard you. They can also determine which roles require which level of access to applications and systems and approve your access.

- **Provisioning:** IGA streamlines the provisioning and de-provisioning of access permissions in an organization at the user level and application level. This automation process can easily be implemented for both on-premises and cloud-based resources, therefore simplifying the IAM management processes.

- **Entitlement management:** Security administrators can use entitlement management capabilities to specify and verify what you are allowed to do when logged into the organization's various applications and systems. For instance, you can be entitled to add, edit, or delete data, while others within the organization are only allowed to view data.

7.3.3 Identity Administration

The identity administration component of IGA systems should incorporate the following elements:

- **Segregation of Duties (SoD):** SoD controls prevent individuals from carrying two or more conflicting functions. For example, you are a loan officer working in a financial institution. You may be prevented from being able to view a corporate bank account and transfer funds to an outside account. This reduces the incidences of a person committing fraud without being discovered. SoD rules can therefore be embedded in multiple systems and across IAM applications.

- **Access reviews:** With the implementation of IGA solutions, an organization is well-placed to streamline the review and verification of user access to various applications and resources. This allows the organization to identify instances of over-provisioning and under-provisioning of access rights as well as simplifying the process of access revocation where necessary. It is crucial to perform access reviews regularly to consider changes in organizational movements.

- **Analytics and reporting:** IGA solutions also provide an organization with visibility of user activities throughout the system. This enables cybersecurity personnel to identify security issues or risks and raise alarms in high-risk situations promptly. The solutions also allow an organization to address policy violations and generate compliance reports.

7.3.4 Challenges in Identity Governance and Administration

Implementing modern IGA solutions can be challenging, and the following are some challenges encountered:

- **Complexity:** The complexity arises from legacy systems that are often incompatible with modern IGA solutions. This makes it difficult to implement a unified IAM framework in an organization. Data will often be housed in silos, and it is challenging to bring all data to a central place.

- **Resistance:** Employees frequently resist changing existing systems to accommodate novel solutions. This is especially pronounced where the changes have the potential to disrupt existing workflows or where the new system introduces cumbersome processes.

- **Short-term resource needs:** Implementing and maintaining a new IGA solution may require more resources upfront, such as time, budget, and skilled employees, to successfully conduct the process. All of these may be lacking in startups and small organizations, thus derailing the implementation processes.

Solutions to the Challenges

An organization can adopt the following solutions to address the above challenges.

- **Automate solutions:** Leverage the automation capabilities of a modern IGA solution to streamline processes. Deploying an organization-wide automated IGA framework reduces administrative and operational burdens.

- **Integrate solutions:** Choose solutions that integrate easily with your current technology stack so you can keep legacy systems that generate value while creating new efficiencies. Ensure that your new modern IGA solution can automatically scale in response to increases in requirements.
- **Get stakeholder buy-in:** Engage key stakeholders early to ensure agreement and support. Offer training, support, and clear communication with employees to better understand the new processes and technologies you are implementing.
- **Monitor:** Continuously monitor and regularly review your IGA processes to facilitate ongoing improvement as you adapt to new compliance requirements and the growing security threat landscape.

7.4 Identity as a Service (IDaaS)

Identity-as-a-Service (IDaaS) is a term referring to a variety of IAM cloud-hosted services. Hosting of IAM components in the cloud protects against cybersecurity attacks targeting such technologies. The cloud is a broad collection of systems and their supporting infrastructure that are accessed over the internet and will be discussed in greater detail in Chapter Nine of this book. IDaaS providers can offer several authentication services, including:

- **Multi-Factor Authentication (MFA):** MFA is the use of multiple authentication factors to verify your identity. One example would require you to insert a USB device into their laptop, besides entering their password. This enhances security compared to just using your username and password.

- **Single-Sign-On (SSO):** SSO allows you to sign up once to a single portal to access all of their SaaS applications, and it also provides a centralized place for companies to manage the applications you have access to as shown in Figure 7.2. Most SSO services are hosted on the cloud and allow you to access their SSO login pages through a web browser.

Figure 7.2 SSO

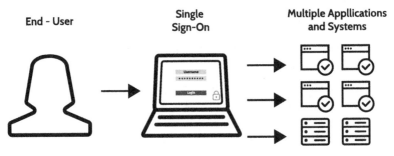

Source: https://blog.systemsengineering.com

- **Identity management:** Identity management activities are undertaken by an Identity Provider (IdP), which is an entity that stores and manages identities. It employs various methods in its operation; it can check identities through associated technologies or may just list the identities with another entity performing the checking processes.

- **Provisioning:** When the system assigns you a role, you will automatically be provisioned to access a role-based IAM solution. This is known as provisioning and extends to the adjustments that are made to your access permissions. IDaaS can be used to automate this process to enhance efficiency and accuracy.

7.4.1 Importance of IDaaS

The right IAM solution assists organizations to effectively and efficiently address complex security challenges as follows:

- **Strengthening security:** Effectively securing IAM systems requires the timely identification of potential exposures, including inappropriate access, policy violations, and unsecured data and applications. The right IDaaS solution can assist organizations in proactively detecting and remediating inappropriate access, strengthening password policies, and eliminating risks.

- **Regulatory compliance:** IDaaS enables organizations to meet their regulatory compliance requirements in terms of security and privacy. IDaaS can replace manual access reviews and certifications with automated tools, thus reducing operational costs.[38] Not only can you significantly reduce the cost of IAM compliance with regulations, but you can also establish repeatable practices for a more consistent, auditable, and secure access certification effort.

- **Cost reduction:** Using a cloud-based IDaaS solution eliminates the need for equipment purchases, specialized IT staff, and ongoing training, allowing your IT team to stay focused on day-to-day operations. A good first impression of a smooth log-in process leads to customer interactions and sales.

- **Better user experience.** SSO can be used in an organization to allow users to log in using a single set of credentials, which enhances the user experience. This also reduces friction and password reset help, which is a

---

38. "What Is Identity-as-a-Service (IDaaS)?," March 3, 2023. https://www.sailpoint.com

cumbersome process. On the same note, MFA can be deployed together to enhance the security setup.
- **Improved Scalability:** As IDaaS solutions are native to the cloud, they are scalable and can be adjusted according to the organization's requirements. This is because cloud-based subscription services adapt easily to changing user requirements, such as an influx of new customers for events and promotions that can be given from time to time.

7.5 Privileged Identity Management (PIM)

Privileged Identity Management (PIM) is a set of security controls that are implemented to monitor, control, and audit access to an organization's privileged identities.[39] Privileged accounts refer to accounts with elevated access to sensitive and critical systems and include service accounts, root users, database accounts, passwords, SSH keys, and digital signatures.

You should note that both PIM and PAM are subsets of identity and access management (IAM). PAM is concerned with the management of privileged access channels and activities throughout an organization. On the other hand, the focus areas for PIM are the effective maintenance of the security controls that are used to manage privileged identities in an organization.

7.5.1 How PIM Works

Figure 7.3 shows a typical example of how a PIM solution works.

---

[39]. "What Is Privileged Identity Management (PIM)? | One Identity." Accessed November 29, 2024. https://www.oneidentity.com

Figure 7.3 How PIM Works

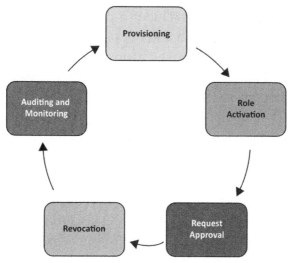

- **Provisioning:** Provisioning is the first step in PIM and involves the creation of roles along with a set of permissions and entitlements. For example, an organization may create Database Administrator roles whose permissions would include the granting of access rights to all the databases in the organization. The roles should be clearly defined to enable authorized identities to easily assume the permissions.
- **Role activation:** This is the stage where the user submits an official request to assume a privileged role in the PIM solution. This request should be time-bound and include the duration and justification for access. The request is placed in an approval workflow that is usually automated.
- **Request approval:** During this stage, the request is approved or denied, depending on a variety of prevailing circumstances. For example, suppose you have requested approval to assume a privileged role, and you have the necessary rights; the PIM solution will

check your credentials. If the approval workflow fails, your request is denied, and a security incident is logged.

- **Revocation of privileges:** Due to a variety of reasons, such as movements within and out of the organization, privileges can be revoked at any given time. The session is terminated upon the revocation of privileges. If you need a session to continue beyond the initially approved duration, you need to send another request to the PIM.

- **Audit and monitoring:** Most PIM tools come with auditing and monitoring capabilities to track and ensure safe use of the provisioned privileged accounts. Cybersecurity administrators can examine audit logs to identify unusual activities and deploy replay mechanisms to investigate suspicious events further, if necessary.

7.5.2 Tips for PIM Implementation

Poor management of privileged accounts may lead to security risks within an organization. Since the privileged accounts have elevated rights, attackers can erase any trace of their actions within the system. Hence, there is a need for greater control over PIM implementation. The following are some tips you can adopt in the implementation of PIM:

- **Perform account discovery:** The first action you need to undertake is to discover all the privileged accounts in the organization. If this is done successfully and thoroughly, it becomes easier to apply PIM principles. This also avoids incidences of privilege creep.

- **Centralize provisioning and storage:** Another important step is to centralize the provisioning and storage of all the discovered privileged accounts. This ensures greater visibility and provides a holistic approach towards the implementation of PIM principles in the organization.

- **Implement RBAC:** It is important to implement RBAC as part of the overall implementation of PIM in an organization. RBAC allows for the implementation of role-based, granular authorization policies for privileged accounts, including the POLP.
- **Enforce strong authentication:** The enforcement of strong authentication practices such as MFA should be a key determinant for a smooth PIM implementation process. It also helps to further secure the PIM environment and make the security environment resilient to threats.
- **Implement Just-in-Time (JIT) access:** The major advantage of JIT in PIM implementation is that it enforces the temporary assignment and revocation of privileges. This is useful when an employee only needs access to a system to perform a single task and should be implemented in PIM as well.
- **Monitor user activities:** Another crucial aspect is the tracking and monitoring of all activity associated with privileged accounts. This helps to enhance the security of privileged accounts and should involve several aspects, including who accesses the systems, when, and the actions that are conducted in the system. Monitoring activities should also include reporting and auditing security-critical events, such as access requests and changes in permissions.

7.6 Emerging Technologies in IAM

The following are some of the emerging trends that are currently relevant in IAM:

- **Passwordless authentication:** Passwordless authentication is any authentication system that eliminates the traditional password-based authentication methods.

It comes in a variety of ways including token-based systems, biometric authentication, or other innovative approaches that eliminate the use of passwords, or any knowledge factors, for that matter, thus enhancing security and simplifying user experience.

- **Biometric authentication:** Biometric authentication is authentication based on inherent biological factors and has revolutionized the way entities prove their identities worldwide. It provides a more robust authentication mechanism compared to passwords, reducing the risk of unauthorized access and eliminating the need to remember complex passwords. It can also be fused with behavioral analytics, which includes physical attributes such as fingerprints and facial recognition, thus creating a robust, personalized authentication process, making impersonation harder for cybercriminals.
- **Adaptive authentication:** This form of authentication represents a paradigm shift in IAM, moving away from static access control models to dynamic and context-aware systems. This trend involves continuously evaluating risk factors in real time, considering variables such as your behavior patterns, geolocation, and device identity. AI facilitates adaptive authentication, dynamically adjusting security measures based on contextual information, user behavior, and risk factors, thus improving the granularity and responsiveness of access controls.
- **Entitlement management:** The management of entitlements is a major issue in IAM current trends. The approach seeks to extend the POLP to ensure that it can adapt to the changes in current emerging technologies. It also incorporates the concept of Just In Time (JIT) access provisioning to ensure that access is only provided for

specific durations. This enhances the security of the IAM environment by preventing the escalation of privileges.

- **IAM in cloud environments:** IAM in cloud environments involves addressing the unique challenges posed by distributed and hybrid cloud architectures. Identity federation, seamless SSO, and secure access control are key aspects of IAM in the cloud. This trend is increased by the flexibility and scalability that cloud services offer, necessitating IAM solutions that can seamlessly operate in these dynamic and diverse environments.

- **Machine Learning (ML) and Artificial Intelligence (AI) in IAM:** The infusion of ML and AI into IAM marks a transformative shift in cybersecurity in the short to medium term. These technologies enable IAM systems to detect anomalies, predict potential security threats, and automate certain processes. ML and AI algorithms can enable identity management systems to analyze large data sets and recognize patterns indicative of both normal and abnormal behavior. The use of AI/ML assists an organization in enhancing its proactiveness in IAM risk management approaches.

- **Decentralized IAM solutions:** Decentralized IAM solutions typically consist of blockchain technologies and these have disrupted the IAM space. They offer decentralized management of identity solutions in an organization, thereby minimizing single points of failure. This reduces the extent of impact should IAM attacks become successful. It also enhances transparency and trust in IAM security operations.

- **Privacy and consent management:** Privacy and consent are some of the topical issues in the IAM industry and, as such, should be given priority in an organization. This is primarily due to recent laws and regulations that seek to protect individual privacy. This trend is likely to increase as individuals are also becoming increasingly aware of their privacy rights, thereby forcing organizations to take steps to align with privacy requirements. This entails that you should implement security processes and procedures while respecting individual privacy rights..

- **Zero-Trust security model:** The Zero Trust approach is another rapidly emerging security practice in IAM. The model requires organizations never to trust users and to continuously verify them before allowing access. Every user request is treated as an attack, unlike the traditional approach of trusting some of the users. The main advantage of the model is that it ensures real-time and continuous assessment of user requests which assists in reducing the overall security risks in an organization.

Chapter Summary

- Identity and access management (IAM) is a discipline of cybersecurity that deals with the identification of users and the management of their access to organizational systems.
- The major components of IAM are identification, authentication, and authorization.
- Authentication factors represent the elements that are used in proving identity and include knowledge, possession, and inherent factors.
- Identity Governance and Administration (IGA) is a security practice that combines identity governance and identity administration to streamline the management of identities in an organization.
- The major advantage and preference in the rise of IDaaS solutions has been their cloud-based nature that allows organizations to reduce operational costs associated with IAM.
- Privileged Identity Management (PIM) provides a set of processes and practices that should be implemented to protect the organization's privileged accounts.
- The cybersecurity industry has witnessed emerging trends in IAM, including decentralized authentication, passwordless authentication, and the adoption of Zero Trust principles.

Quiz

1. Which of the following elements is ordinarily not part of an organization's IAM strategy aimed at enhancing the security of its digital identities?
   a. Identification
   b. Authentication
   c. Authorization
   d. Encryption

2. You attempt to log in to a system by providing your username. Which of the following steps in the IAM process are you performing?
   a. Authentication
   b. Authorization
   c. Identification
   d. Accountability

3. Your organization would like to implement a more secure login method by requiring a password and a one-time code that is sent to the user's mobile phone. Which of the following refers to this form of authentication?
   a. Single-Factor Authentication (SFA)
   b. Two-Factor Authentication (2FA)
   c. Multi-Factor Authentication (MFA)
   d. Dual-Based Authentication (KBA)

4. An organization seeks to allow employee access to its sensitive data during work hours only. Which of the following types of access control would you advise the organization to implement?
   a. Role-Based Access Control (RBAC)
   b. Attribute-Based Access Control (ABAC)
   c. Mandatory Access Control (MAC)
   d. Discretionary Access Control (DAC)

5. Which of the following methods would you advise the system administrator to implement to enforce centrally defined access control policies across all organizational systems users?
   a. Role-Based Access Control (RBAC)
   b. Attribute-Based Access Control (ABAC)
   c. Mandatory Access Control (MAC)
   d. Discretionary Access Control (DAC)

6. Your organization has decided to use biometric authentication to verify the identities of its employees. Which of the following types of authentication factors does this approach represent?
   a. Knowledge factor
   b. Possession factor
   c. Inherent factor
   d. Authorization factor

7. During a recent cybersecurity review in your organization, you discover that one of the junior-level cybersecurity analysts can view firewall configurations but cannot make changes. Which of the following is being implemented?
   a. Role-Based Access Control (RBAC)
   b. Attribute-Based Access Control (ABAC)
   c. Mandatory Access Control (MAC)
   d. Discretionary Access Control (DAC)

8. What is the main purpose of incorporating Identity Governance and Administration (IGA) solutions as a part of an organization's overall IAM strategy?
   a. To support authentication
   b. To govern and administer digital identities
   c. To deploy encryption services efficiently
   d. To monitor the security of network traffic

9. Which of the following infrastructures do IDaaS solutions leverage?
   a. Cloud
   b. Physical
   c. Network
   d. Data center

10. Which part of IGA solutions is concerned with the formulation of policies and procedures that guide the operations of digital identities in an organization?
    a. Identity governance
    b. Identity administration
    c. Identity provisioning
    d. Identity monitoring

Answers

| 1 – d | 2 – c | 3 – b | 4 – b | 5 – c |
| 6 – c | 7 – a | 8 – b | 9 – a | 10 – a |

CHAPTER 8
Security Testing

Key Learning Objectives
- Identifying threats and security weaknesses on time
- Prioritizing threats for remediation
- Addressing security gaps and protecting sensitive systems and information
- Meeting cybersecurity compliance and regulatory needs and avoiding penalties

One of the best practices in cybersecurity is to schedule regular, automated scans of all critical IT systems. This allows you to review an organization's security posture to identify, prioritize, and remediate potential vulnerabilities that could expose you to cyber threats or risks. Refer to the OWASP™ Top 10 Resource provided in the online resources section of this book to better understand the concepts covered in this chapter.

8.1 Vulnerability Assessments

Imagine a situation where you are unaware of any weaknesses within your systems, only for threats to exploit them when you are unprepared. No business will want to be in such a situation. The best would be to always be on top of your organization's security weaknesses and take measures to address them before attackers exploit them. That is the essence of vulnerability assessment.

A vulnerability assessment is a systematic review of security weaknesses or loopholes in an information system. The purpose is to evaluate the system's susceptibility to known vulnerabilities. The process also assigns severity levels to discover vulnerabilities and recommends remediation actions.

8.1.1 Types of Vulnerability Scans

You should be familiar with the common types of vulnerability scans, including the following:

- **Network-based scans:** You can conduct network-based scans to discover vulnerabilities in your network's infrastructure and devices such as routers, switches, and firewalls. It helps you to discover outdated firmware, improper configurations, and other potential weaknesses in your network's defenses.

- **Host-based scans:** A host is any device in an organization that runs some applications, such as an email server or a database. Host-based scans focus on discovering vulnerabilities in individual systems or devices, installed software, and system configurations among other hosts. For example, a host-based scan can discover systems with an outdated version of an operating system with known vulnerabilities.

- **Wireless network scans:** These scans are conducted to discover vulnerabilities in wireless networks, including weaknesses in encryption, authentication, and network configurations. These scans are very useful to a cybersecurity professional, as wireless networks can often provide an easier point of entry than wired networks.
- **Application scans:** These scans focus on identifying vulnerabilities in specific applications, including web applications, mobile applications, and other software. They can discover weaknesses, such as cross-site scripting vulnerabilities and SQL injection vulnerabilities.
- **Database scans:** The focus of database scans is identifying database weaknesses, such as issues to do with database configuration, outdated database software, improper access controls, and vulnerability to injection attacks.

8.1.2 The Vulnerability Assessment Process

The vulnerability assessment process comprises four critical steps, namely testing, analysis, assessment, and remediation, as shown in Figure 8.1.

Figure 8.1 Vulnerability Assessment Process

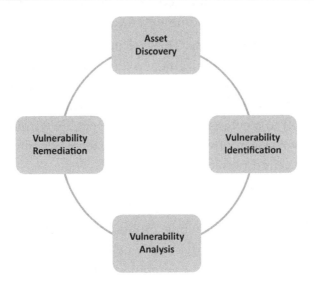

- **Asset discovery:** The initial stage in the vulnerability assessment process is for you to discover the IT assets to assess. This involves identifying and cataloguing all IT assets in use in the organization, including hardware equipment, networking equipment, software applications, and cloud-based assets.
- **Vulnerability identification:** During this stage, also known as vulnerability scanning, you draft a comprehensive list of an application's vulnerabilities. While the scanning can be undertaken using manual methods, you can leverage numerous automated tools available in the market to perform the scanning process. This speeds up the process and leads to more accurate results.
- **Vulnerability analysis:** During this stage, you identify the source and root cause of the vulnerabilities identified in the first stage. You particularly need to identify the system components responsible for each vulnerability, as well as the root cause of the vulnerability. For

example, the root cause of a vulnerability can be an outdated version of the operating system.

- **Vulnerability remediation:** The objective of this step is to close security gaps as well as to reduce attack surfaces. This includes minimizing all the possible points in an organization where unauthorized access can occur. Specific remediation steps might include updating procedures and applying security patches.

For example, you can carry out a vulnerability assessment on a web application. You identify your web application in the asset discovery phase. You then choose a tool to perform the assessment; in this case, say you choose Nessus. Nessus is a vulnerability scanner similar to OpenVAS, Qualys, and Burp Suite. Normally, you would need the web or IP address of the web application, and you enter these into Nessus. Nessus will scan and produce the results of all the vulnerabilities identified alongside their scores and recommended actions to address them. The next step for you would be to apply the recommendations to remediate the vulnerabilities and then perform a rescan. If all the recommendations are applied appropriately, the rescan will produce a clean result.

8.1.3 Vulnerability Assessment Tools

The vulnerability assessment process typically involves the use of automated tools to automatically scan for new and existing threats. Types of vulnerability assessment tools include:

- **Web application scanners:** These are used to simulate known attack patterns targeting web applications.

- **Protocol scanners:** Protocol scanners are deployed to search for vulnerable protocols, ports, and network services in an organization's networks.
- **Network scanners:** You can use network scanners to gain greater visibility in your network environment and discover warning signals of potential vulnerabilities. These signals can range from stray IP addresses to spoofed packets.

8.1.4 Vulnerability Assessments vs. Vulnerability Scanning

As a cybersecurity professional, you should understand the difference between vulnerability assessment and vulnerability scanning. Below is an explanation of the slight difference between the two concepts:

- **Vulnerability assessment:** A vulnerability assessment is a proactive comprehensive process that includes identifying, documenting, and providing guidance for remediating vulnerabilities.
- **Vulnerability scanning:** Vulnerability scanning is a part of the vulnerability assessment process and involves the application of automated tools to scan systems for known vulnerabilities.

8.1.5 Challenges in Vulnerability Assessment

The following are some of the main challenges you encounter when performing a vulnerability assessment within an organization:

- **Challenges with accuracy:** These include both false positives and false negatives. A false positive in a vulnerability assessment refers to a situation where a vulnerability that does not exist is flagged by the system, while a false negative is when a real vulnerability goes undetected. False positives can lead to a waste of resources resolving non-existent threats, while with false negatives, the system is exposed to potential cyber-attacks.

- **Emerging vulnerabilities:** Cybersecurity professionals also face the risk of having to keep pace with emerging vulnerabilities. This is because the cybersecurity landscape is ever-evolving, with new vulnerabilities and threats cropping up. Cybersecurity teams must regularly update vulnerability assessment tools and the threat intelligence they rely on. For example, you need to add tools that can scan for vulnerabilities in cloud and containerized environments, as these are newer technologies associated with emerging vulnerabilities.
- **Environmental complexities:** Hybrid environments and containerized platforms present unique challenges in vulnerability assessments. A hybrid environment consists of an organization operating on-premises and in the cloud at the same time, while a containerized environment consists of entire software packages that are necessary for running an application. The diversity in these systems, from legacy to modern architectures, makes it difficult to devise a unified scanning strategy, which also requires specialized tools.

8.1.6 Best Practices for Vulnerability Assessment

While executing a vulnerability assessment does come with its challenges, the following practices will assist you in simplifying the process and increasing its effectiveness:

- **Adopt continuous scanning:** Vulnerabilities can arise at any time due to various factors, such as the introduction of new software or hardware, configuration changes, or the discovery of new threats. Conducting regular vulnerability assessments, ideally on a quarterly basis, is vital in maintaining system security.[40]

- **Customize scanning profiles:** You can develop customized scanning profiles that are tailored to their specific systems and applications. This includes consideration of factors such as the criticality of the assets being scanned and legal requirements. This approach allows for a more accurate and comprehensive assessment, as it prioritizes vulnerabilities based on their severity and potential impact. This enables the effective allocation of resources, focusing on the most critical vulnerabilities first.

- **Update asset inventory:** You should ensure that the inventory of all systems, applications, and devices is kept up to date. This allows you to know what is in your environment and understand the potential vulnerabilities each element may have, enabling you to prioritize the vulnerabilities based on their criticality.

- **Involve cross-functional teams:** Involving cross-functional teams ensures collaboration which assists in ensuring no aspects are overlooked, allowing you to discover vulnerabilities more comprehensively. The assessment should include IT, security, operations, software development, and business units, with each team bringing its own perspective and expertise.

---

40. CyCognito. "Vulnerability Assessment: Process, Challenges & Best Practices." Accessed December 17, 2024. https://www.cycognito.com

8.2 Penetration Tests

Penetration testing (Pentest for short) is a simulated security exercise where a cyber-security expert attempts to find and exploit vulnerabilities in a computer system that attackers could take advantage of. This is like hiring someone to act as a burglar and try to break into your house. If the 'burglar' succeeds and gets into the house, you will get valuable information on how to strengthen your security measures.

8.2.1 Importance of Penetration Testing

Penetration testing is a key element in the whole cybersecurity framework of operations as it provides important benefits in enhancing the security posture of an organization. Some of these advantages include the following:

- **Discovery of vulnerabilities and flaws:** Penetration testing helps you to discover vulnerabilities and flaws in their systems that they might not have otherwise been able to find. This can help stop attacks before they start, as you can fix these vulnerabilities once they have been identified.

- **Regulatory compliance:** The exercise can help you comply with data security and privacy regulations by finding ways that sensitive data could be exposed. For instance, PCI DSS version 4.0 requires you to use penetration testing.

- **Improved security:** As a result of penetration tests, you are better placed to address loopholes in your cybersecurity assurance practices, such as automated tools, configuration and coding standards, architecture analysis, and other lighter-weight vulnerability assessment activities.

8.2.2 Categories of Penetration Tests

The following are some of the major categories of penetration tests.

- **Application penetration tests:** These detect vulnerabilities in applications, including web applications, cloud applications, and application programming interfaces (APIs). You may need to reference the OWASP™ Top 10, a list of the most critical vulnerabilities in web applications, as part of your penetration testing exercise. The OWASP™ Top 10 list is provided as part of the online resources available with this book.

- **Network penetration tests:** Network penetration tests exploit an organization's entire computer network and include external tests and internal tests. In external tests, penetration testers mimic the behavior of external hackers to discover security issues, while in internal tests, penetration testers mimic the behavior of malicious insiders, such as insiders abusing access privileges to steal sensitive data.

- **Hardware penetration tests:** These search for vulnerabilities in devices connected to the network as well as the network infrastructure itself. Penetration testers may discover software flaws or physical vulnerabilities such as an improperly secured data center.

- **Personnel penetration tests:** These are used to identify weaknesses in employees' cybersecurity hygiene. They assess how vulnerable an organization is to social engineering attacks.

8.2.3 Types of Penetration Tests

Though the terms penetration tests and penetration categories are sometimes used interchangeably, you need to be sure not to confuse the two. Penetration categories are collections of penetration tests that can be carried out, while types of penetration tests are the various forms the tests can take, including the following:

- **Black box:** The penetration tester does not know anything about the internal structure of the target system and, therefore, acts as an attacker. The process involves probing for any externally exploitable weaknesses. Penetration testers have to rely on their research to develop an attack plan, as a real-world hacker would.
- **Grey box:** In a grey box, the penetration tester possesses some knowledge of one or more sets of credentials and the target's internal data structures, code, and algorithms. It is, therefore, possible for the penetration tester to construct test cases of the target system based on detailed design documents.
- **White box:** Penetration testers have total visibility into the target system.[41] Hence, this method is sometimes referred to as transparent testing. You will share all system details, such as network diagrams, source codes, and credentials, with the penetration tester.

8.2.4 Penetration Testing Process

Figure 8.2 below shows a typical penetration testing process in an organization according to Hack the Box (HTB[42]).

---

41. Wali Hasib. "What Is Penetration Testing in Cyber Security." Website & Software Development With Advance Cyber Security (blog), August 27, 2024. https://zerobugsbd.com

42. Academy, H. T. B. "Penetration Testing Process Course | HTB Academy." Accessed June 11, 2025. https://academy.hackthebox.com/course/preview/penetration-testing-process

Figure 8.2 Penetration Testing Process

- **Pre-engagement:** During this stage the penetration tester and the client meet to set the scope of the test, discuss the objectives of the test and set the rules. This is crucial in setting boundaries and avoiding issues during the test.
- **Information gathering:** Penetration tests start with a phase of reconnaissance, during which an ethical hacker gathers data and information that they will use to plan their simulated attack. You should also ensure that you obtain management consent before undertaking any penetration test. This is because any penetration test conducted without management approval may be regarded as a criminal act.
- **Vulnerability assessment:** Penetration testers use tools to examine the target website or system for weaknesses, including open services, application security issues, and open-source vulnerabilities. Penetration testers can deploy a variety of scanning depending on the results of

the reconnaissance stage and new information obtained during the testing process.
- **Exploitation:** The testing team begins the actual attack. Penetration testers try a variety of attacks depending on the target system, the vulnerabilities they found, and the scope of the test. They exploit a vulnerability to get a foothold in the system and laterally move within the network. For example, they might start by planting a keylogger on an employee's computer to capture the employee's credentials.
- **Post-exploitation:** The penetration tester wraps up the test by covering their tracks; this means removing any embedded hardware to avoid detection. This involves cleaning up all traces. Penetration testers prepare a report on the attack outlining the vulnerabilities discovered, the exploits used, and details on their actions inside the system. The report may also include specific recommendations on vulnerability remediations.
- **Lateral movement:** During this stage the tester will move from compromised machines to other areas within the network. This method is often used in red team exercises to determine the extent of the weaknesses within the network.
- **Proof of concept:** The penetration tester provides evidence of the parts of the organizational networks that can be exploited. This enables the organization to make informed decisions regarding remediation.
- **Post-engagement:** The penetration tester provides a report and briefs the client about the test. The report includes recommendations and an option retesting after the vulnerabilities have been remediated.

8.2.5 Penetration Testing Tools

There is no one-size-fits-all tool for penetration tools as they come in different penetration tests:

- **Specialized operating systems:** Most penetration testers use OSs designed for penetration testing and ethical hacking, such as Kali Linux. Kali Linux is an open-source Linux distribution that comes pre-installed with penetration testing tools like Nmap, Wireshark, and Metasploit.

- **Credential-cracking tools:** These tools are deployed to uncover passwords by breaking encryptions or launching brute-force attacks. They use bots or scripts to automatically generate and test potential passwords until one works. Examples include Hashcat and John the Ripper.

- **Port scanners:** Port scanners allow penetration testers to remotely test devices for open and available ports. These tools are used to simulate how attackers can breach a network. Nmap is the most widely used port scanner in the marketplace.

8.2.6 Vulnerability Assessments vs. Penetration Tests

As a cybersecurity professional, you should be careful to be able to differentiate vulnerability assessments from penetration tests and advise the organization appropriately. While there are similarities, these methods serve slightly different purposes. The best approach is to employ both methods as they complement each other. Table 8.1 below shows the main differences between these two methods of security testing.

Table 8.1 Differences Between Vulnerability Assessments and Penetration Tests

Aspect	Vulnerability assessments	Penetration tests
Comprehensiveness	Vulnerability assessments are less comprehensive than penetration tests and just discover weaknesses.	Penetration tests are more comprehensive and exploit identified vulnerabilities.
Frequency	Vulnerability assessments are typically recurring, automated scans that search for known vulnerabilities in a system and flag them for review.	Penetration tests are periodic, usually undertaken every quarter or when significant changes occur in an organization.
Service provider	Vulnerability assessment is conducted by in-house personnel.	Penetration testing services are provided by third-party security experts who approach the systems from the perspective of an attacker.

8.3 Dynamic Testing

We have discussed vulnerability assessments and penetration testing in the previous sections, but our discussion will not be comprehensive without touching on code testing. This is because the code itself, if not properly tested, can lead to a variety of security vulnerabilities. There are two main methods of code testing, namely, dynamic testing and static testing.

Dynamic testing is used to test code behavior during runtime. The process involves providing the software with input and validating its output. Its objective is to check if the software is performing as it is supposed to.

8.3.1 Methods of Dynamic Testing

The following are brief explanations of the major methods used in the dynamic testing process:

- **Black-box testing:** In a black-box test, you test the software's functionalities without any knowledge of its internal workings. As a tester, you just input the data and check if the output meets your expectations.

- **White-box testing:** During a white-box test, you obtain the software's internal implementation details before performing the test. This information includes the software's internal functions, methods, or code snippets.

- **Grey-box testing:** In grey-box testing, you combine the black-box and white-box testing methods. This means that you will possess partial knowledge of the internal workings of the software. This method allows you to develop more comprehensive test cases.

- **Regression testing:** You conduct regression testing when you intend to add new features to existing software and wish to ensure that those changes do not impact existing features negatively. It involves testing all items, selecting a regression test and prioritizing test cases as shown in Figure 8.3.

Figure 8.3   Regression Testing

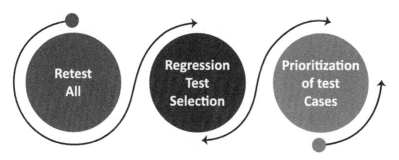

Source: https://cloudnineitservices.com

- **Performance testing:** A performance test evaluates the software's performance aspects, such as response time, load capacity, and stability. This test allows you to ensure that the software you are developing can handle real-world situations.
- **Security testing:** Security testing is crucial to ensuring that the newly developed software is safe and secure from malicious attacks such as data breaches and unauthorized access.

8.4 Static Testing

Static testing is a type of testing that you perform without executing the actual code to identify any bugs, errors, and vulnerabilities.[43] During testing, you review and validate the product and its supporting documents. This is different from dynamic testing where you carry out the test during code execution.

---

43. madeline. "Static Testing: What You Need to Know." Cprime, May 12, 2021. https://www.cprime.com

8.4.1 Importance of Static Testing

Static testing is performed due to its ability to provide important benefits to an organization, including the following:

- **Improved productivity:** One of the key benefits of static testing is that it improves the productivity of the software development teams by reducing the incidence of flaws during the development process.
- **Reduced costs:** Static testing also reduces the number of defects found later in the software development process. This contributed to a reduction in the entire software testing costs.
- **Early bugs detection:** Static testing assists you in detecting bugs during the early stages of the software development process. This makes it less time-consuming and costly to fix the identified bugs.
- **Improved software quality:** Overall, static testing enhances the overall software quality of the software product by ensuring compliance with the coding standards and best practices.

8.4.2 Static Testing Techniques

Static testing consists of two major techniques, namely, review and static analysis.

- **Review:** During a review, your main aim is to discover potential defects in the design of the software. Once you detect the errors, you can proceed to remove them in the various software documentation such as software requirements specifications. Personnel can examine the documents and remove any identified errors, redundancies, and ambiguities. The review process is conducted in four main ways, as follows.

- **Informal:** During an informal review, as the creator of the documents, you vail them to the audience and provide everyone with an opportunity to give their opinion. This enables you to detect defects during the early stages of software development.
- **Walkthrough:** A walkthrough is performed by an experienced cybersecurity expert. The expert checks defects to reduce the incidence of problems in the subsequent software development stages.
- **Peer review:** During a peer review, the tester reviews documents one after the other to detect defects. Defects should be fixed upon detection to reduce risks associated with their prevalence. You should note that a peer review is usually carried out in a team setting.
- **Inspection:** Inspection involves the verification of documents by the higher authority in an organization, such as the CISO or CTO. A good example of inspection is the verification of the software requirement specifications (SRS) document by the CTO.
- **Static Analysis:** Static analysis involves the evaluation of the code quality that is written by software developers. It leverages a variety of tools to carry out code analysis against a certain standard. Through static analysis, you are better placed to identify the following defects:
  - Unused variables
  - Dead code
  - Infinite loops
  - Variable with an undefined value
  - Wrong syntax

8.4.3 Static Testing vs Dynamic Testing

Table 8.2 below summarises the major differences between static testing and dynamic testing, which you should know as a cybersecurity professional.

Table 8.2 Differences Between Static Testing and Dynamic Testing

Aspect	Static testing	Dynamic testing
Testing objective	The objective of static testing is to prevent defects.	The objective of dynamic testing is to detect defects.
Verification and validation dynamics	Static testing is part of the verification process and is carried out before the development of the system.	Dynamic testing is part of the validation process and is conducted after the development of the system.
Problem rectification	Rectifying the issues at the initial stage reduces the cost and time.	Rectifying the issues is a long process and does not lead to a reduction in cost and time.
Test mechanism	The test is carried out without executing the actual source code of the application.[44]	The test is conducted after executing the programming code of the application.

8.5 Secure Coding Practices

Cybersecurity professionals should ensure that developers adhere to secure coding practices to reduce the risk of security vulnerabilities in applications. The OWASP™ Top 10

---

44. BrowserStack. "What Is Static Testing?" Accessed December 17, 2024. https://browserstack.wpengine.com

reveals that a considerable number of the vulnerabilities in software emanate from poor coding practices.[45] Table 8.3 below shows some of the secure coding practices that should be observed during software development.

Table 8.3   Secure Coding Practices

Aspect	Validation Steps
Input validation	• Ensure all your input is sanitized. • Carry out input validation using trusted systems. • Validate all data from untrusted sources. • Employ a centralized input validation routine covering the whole application. • Reject all input that experiences validation failure.
Output encoding	• Encode all your output on a trusted system. • Use a standard routine for output encoding. A good example is UTF.[46] • Sanitize all output before use.
Authentication	• Enforce a strong authentication such as MFA. • Establish and use standard, tested, and consistent authentication services. • Use centralized authentication systems for authentication solutions.
Session management	• Configure and use server session management controls. • Utilise vetted algorithms for session management controls. • Encrypt all sensitive information using strong encryption protocols such as TLS.

---

45. "OWASP Top Ten | OWASP Foundation." Accessed December 25, 2024. https://owasp.org
46. OWASP Secure Coding Practices - Quick Reference Guide | Secure Coding Practices | OWASP Foundation." Accessed December 17, 2024. https://owasp.org

Aspect	Validation Steps
Access control	• Use only trusted system objects for making access authorization decisions. • Ensure that access controls fail securely. • Ensure that privileged logic is separate from the application code. • Implement the POLP to restrict access to files or other resources.
Error handling	• Avoid disclosing sensitive information in error responses, including system details and session identifiers. • Ensure that error handlers do not display debugging or other sensitive information. • Ensure the application can handle application errors and does not rely on the server configuration. • Properly free-allocated memory upon the occurrence of errors.

Chapter Summary

- A cybersecurity professional should be able to perform security testing to test vulnerabilities and the resilience of the organization's systems to withstand information security attacks if they were to materialize.
- The two major forms of security testing are vulnerability scanning and penetration testing.
- Cybersecurity professionals should be proficient in performing vulnerability assessments and penetration tests of organizational systems and be able to interpret the results for the benefit of the organization's decision-making bodies.
- A variety of automated tools can be used to perform vulnerability scans and penetration tests, each with its own merits and demerits. A thorough analysis is therefore required before adopting and using such tools.
- Cybersecurity professionals should always seek management approval to undertake any penetration test, as testing without approval may be viewed as a criminal activity.
- Static testing involves testing code in static mode, that is, when not executing. On the other hand, dynamic testing is testing code in runtime, that is, while it executes.
- In a black box test, the tester has no prior knowledge of the software under test while in a white box test, the tester is provided with all the information, including the internal working of the software.
- The OWASP™ Top 10 reveals that poor coding practices are a major cause of insecure software. This calls for increased adoption of secure coding practices within organizations.

Quiz

1. Sam is the IT manager at your organization. He would like to discover vulnerabilities in the organization's network infrastructure and devices and has approached you for advice. Which of the following scans will you advise him to undertake?

    a. Host-based scan
    b. Network-based scan
    c. Application scan
    d. Database scan

2. Which of the following scans focuses on identifying vulnerabilities in an organization's wireless network encryption and authentication?

    a. Infrastructure scan
    b. Application scan
    c. Network-based scan
    d. Wireless network scan

3. Which of the following processes is associated with the resolution of identified vulnerabilities?

    a. Analysis
    b. Execution
    c. Containment
    d. Remediation

4. A cybersecurity analyst discovers that several systems in your organization have outdated operating systems. Which stage of the vulnerability assessment process does this represent?
   a. Asset discovery
   b. Vulnerability identification
   c. Threat assessment
   d. Vulnerability remediation

5. The IT department would like to assess the impact of each of the identified vulnerabilities. Which of these represents this stage in the vulnerability assessment process?
   a. Asset discovery
   b. Vulnerability identification
   c. Vulnerability analysis
   d. Vulnerability remediation

6. You would like to simulate known attack patterns targeting your organization's applications. Which of the vulnerability assessment tools would you deploy for this purpose?
   a. Protocol scanner
   b. Network scanner
   c. Web application scanner
   d. Device scanner

7. Which of the vulnerability assessment tools would you recommend for an organization seeking to discover potential vulnerabilities, such as spoofed packets?
   a. Protocol scanner
   b. Network scanner
   c. Web application scanner
   d. Database scanner

8. You notice that you are experiencing false positives in your vulnerability assessments, leading to wasted resources. Which of the following challenges are you encountering?
   a. Emerging vulnerabilities
   b. Skill challenges
   c. Challenges with accuracy
   d. Poor planning

9. Which of the following security exercises is associated with the hiring of a security expert to act like a malicious outsider and try to exploit vulnerabilities in organizational systems?
   a. Vulnerability scanning
   b. Stealth testing
   c. Penetration testing
   d. Protocol scanning

10. The penetration test team at your organization has informed you that they will focus on finding vulnerabilities in web applications, APIs, and cloud applications. What form of penetration is the team planning to undertake?
   a. Network
   b. Host
   c. Application
   d. Endpoint

Answers

1 – b	2 – d	3 – d	4 – b	5 – c
6 – c	7 – a	8 – c	9 – c	10 – c

CHAPTER 9
Incident Management

Key Learning Objectives
- Detect cyber incidents happening in an organization on time
- Prioritize incidents to determine which issues to address first
- Contain and eradicate incidents
- Learn from incidents and assist in enhancing the overall security posture

Incident response management allows you to detect, analyze, contain, eradicate, and recover from an incident. These incidents range from minor attacks such as malware infections to sophisticated attacks such as ransomware, social engineering attacks, and DoS attacks. This chapter discusses the major aspects of what you need to know about incident management in an organization.

9.1 Incident Response Process

The National Institute of Standards and Technology (NIST) incident response lifecycle breaks incident response down into four main phases, namely: preparation; detection and analysis; containment, eradication, and recovery; and post-event activity, as shown in Figure 9.1 below.[47]

Figure 9.1 Incident Response Process

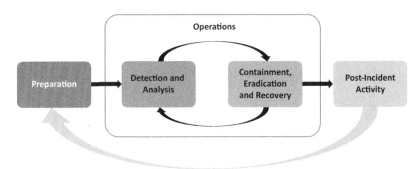

Source: https://docs.aws.amazon.com

Below are brief explanations of the NIST Incident Response Stages depicted in Figure 9.1:

- **Preparation:** During this phase, an organization will work towards getting ready for effective incident response processes. This involves the setting, crafting, and implementation of incident response policies and procedures, the setting up of the Incident Response Team (IRT) and other teams to support the incident response process. It also encompasses the establishment of the right tools and resources, including the required training for the teams.

---

47. National Institute of Standards and Technology (COR). *Computer Security Incident Handling Guide*. Createspace Independent Pub 2013., 2013.

- **Detection and analysis:** The detection and analysis phase is concerned with accurately detecting and assessing incidents in an organization. For cybersecurity professionals, failure to properly detect and analyze cyber incidents can result in the deployment of wrong incident responses. You should, therefore, ensure that you have properly detected and analyzed every incident for effective results.
- **Containment, eradication, and recovery:** This phase consists of focusing on reducing the impact of an incident, completely removing the incident, and enabling the recovery of business operations. It encompasses three major aspects as follows:
  - **Containment:** Containment means preventing the incident from spreading laterally within organizational systems. You should implement all the possible methods and mechanisms available to prevent the spread of the detected incidents. For example, to prevent malware from spreading, you may need to block traffic to and from the infected IP addresses.
  - **Eradication:** Containing is not sufficient as the incident is still resident in organizational systems. Therefore, after containing the incident, you would need to go a step further to eradicate the incident and its causes from your computer environment. In the case of malware, you will need to remove the malware from all your systems.
  - **Recovery:** Once incidents are contained and eradicated, you enter into recovery mode. This stage involves restoring all systems to their pre-incident state so that they begin to function normally. This process involves a lot of activities, including restoring data from backups, rebuilding damaged systems,

and re-enabling disabled accounts to allow teams to continue operations.

Take note of the arrows in Figure 9.1. During the operations phase, activities will often cycle back to detection as more information is gathered during the containment, eradication, and recovery phases. For example, while eradicating a malware infection at a particular endpoint, you may realise that more endpoints are affected, causing you to carry out further analyses. And, of course, the lessons learned will feed into the next cycle of the incident response process.

- **Post-incident activity:** After an incident you need to do a review of the root causes of the incident and how you handled it. This is one of the critical but often overlooked phases in the incident response process, as learning from incidents allows you to perfect your incident response processes going forward. Basically, during the post-incident activities stage, you perform a sort of postmortem exercise of the entire incident. This assists you in understanding how the incident took place as well as how to prevent such incidents from happening in the future.

9.2 Tips for Improving an Incident Response

There are many ways in which you can improve the effectiveness of your incident response processes, including the following:

- **Invest in security training:** You must train incident handlers to be always prepared in case of incidents. The rest of the employees would also need to know their responsibilities when an incident occurs, which may vary across differing roles and responsibilities. This includes things like when to report an incident, who to contact, and the tools available for containing the incident.[48]

- **Establish effective communication:** Effective communication processes and channels are also key to creating an effective incident response process in an organization. This enables teams to respond to their assigned contact in a swift manner, thus ensuring a smooth and quick process in detecting and recovering from incidents.

- **Monitor response actions:** It is crucial for you to monitor activity and maintain logs for each system and update them regularly, leaving no gaps in the data. Logging allows you to pinpoint the sources of incidents affecting your organization, thus assisting you in devising strategies to prevent similar incidents from occurring in the future.

- **Perform regular tests:** Regularly test the incident response plan so that the documentation stays up to date with any changes made to security policies or new technologies introduced to the organization's infrastructure.

- **Invest in a Security Operations Center (SOC):** While onsite presence and real-time availability is ideal for enabling immediate responses, you may need to invest in a remote SOC as well to reduce costs associated with commuting. However, this also usually comes at a huge cost in terms of laying out the initial infrastructure.

- **Hire security experts:** You should note that incident response requires expertise and knowledge of communication protocols, IT systems, attack techniques, and the organization's systems, procedures, and

---

[48]. Praveen. "Understanding the Incident Response Life Cycle." *Cybersecurity Exchange* (blog), March 30, 2022. https://www.eccouncil.org

environments.[49] The best approach is to outsource skilled personnel while also retaining internal employees as they have a better understanding of the organization's IT environment.

9.3 Business Continuity and Disaster Recovery (BCDR)

Business Continuity Disaster Recovery (BCDR) refers to all those processes that are carried out to enable an organization to return to normal operations after having experienced a disaster. It is one of the most critical elements that should be the focus of cybersecurity professionals because any failure to resume operations on time may prove catastrophic to the organization. As a cybersecurity professional, you should ensure that BCDR operations are properly functioning to enhance availability in an organization.

Most organizations divide their BCDR activities into two separate processes: business continuity and disaster recovery. This is generally seen as an effective approach because these two processes share many characteristics, even though there are some differences. The typical BCDR process is depicted in Figure 9.2.

---

49. BlueVoyant. "NIST Incident Response: Framework and Key Recommendations." Accessed December 24, 2024. https://www.bluevoyant.com

Figure 9.2 The BCDR Process

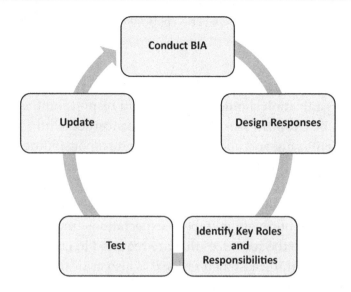

These stages are explained below:

- **Perform a Business Impact Analysis (BIA):** BIA refers to the process of identifying and evaluating the risks an organization is exposed to and the potential impact of a disaster on normal business operations. It generally incorporates an overview of all potential existing threats and vulnerabilities, their likelihood, and their impact. Carrying out a BIA allows an organization to identify and understand the risks that the organization faces in its operations.

- **Design responses:** Once the organization has completed the BIA, the next stage in the BCDR policy is to plan effective responses to every threat that has been identified in the BIA stage. When evaluating the organization's BCDR responses, the cybersecurity professional should appreciate that different threats would require different disaster recovery strategies and that there is no one-size-fits-all approach in designing responses. The responses should detail how the organization will approach a specific threat and mitigate it.

- **Identify key roles and responsibilities.** Members of the organization should have roles and responsibilities in BCDR processes. This stage is concerned with identifying and allocating roles and responsibilities to organizational members and selecting the key people to be involved. Members should be well-acquainted with how they will respond in times of disaster. The stage documents every member's expectations from others and also the resources that are required to effectively carry out the assigned tasks. It is also critical to lay down the communication processes to be followed by the members when a disaster occurs.

- **Test:** The organization is not in a position to know whether the BCDR plan and process would work without subjecting the plan to a test. Therefore, the organization should continuously test its plan in real-life simulation exercises and other methods. This will help the organization gauge the plan's relevance and the behavior of the members in times of disaster. Testing also enables the team to gain confidence in acting in their respective roles and responsibilities.

- **Update:** Based on the results of the test, the organization should update its plan to move with the times and maintain relevance. This stage presents the organization with an opportunity to refine the plan in terms of roles, responsibilities, and resources required, among other critical elements.

9.4 Disaster Recovery

A disaster is an emergency event of such great magnitude that it overwhelms the capacity to respond and takes considerable time from which to recover. It is different from an incident because an incident typically causes a minor disruption and can be contained and eradicated. A disaster, on the other hand, is a catastrophic disruption that may bring the entire IT operation down. The following terms are critical to an understanding of disaster recovery activities in an organization:

- **Disaster Recovery (DR):** We can view disaster recovery as the ability of an organization to respond to disasters. A disaster is different from an incident, therefore, each would require its plan. In this case, you will need a Disaster Recovery Plan (DRP) to guide in restoring your critical business functions.

- **Disaster Recovery Plan (DRP):** A DRP covers all the processes, procedures, and resources that are implemented in an organization to recover, within a defined time and cost, an activity that has been affected by a disaster. The DRP can be maintained as a separate document or combined with a BCP.

- **Disaster declaration:** Declaring a disaster is crucial in disaster recovery to enable the execution of the next step. If a disaster is not declared, no one will know it has happened, and the provisions of the DRP will remain mute. Therefore, there is a need to designate an individual who declares a disaster so that action can commence if a disaster strikes. This individual will also be responsible for ensuring communications to appropriate internal and external parties that the DRP is being put into operation.

- **Recovery Point Objective (RPO):** The RPO is the earliest point in time that is acceptable to recover data for the organization. It represents the amount of data that the organization can afford to lose in a disaster.

- **Recovery Time Objective (RTO):** This refers to the length of time it takes to restore a business process or function after an unplanned incident or disaster occurs. The RTO should be as short as possible, as you would not want to take a long time in disaster mode.

9.4.1 Importance of Disaster Recovery

There are several reasons why an organization should embark on a BCDR strategy and why the cybersecurity professional should ensure that the organization's BCDR processes and activities are properly designed and working as intended. Some of the reasons why BCDR is important include the following:

- **Enhances risk mitigation:** BCDR helps mitigate risks associated with unexpected events such as natural disasters, cyberattacks, or system failures. Planning for disasters allows you to minimize the impact of disruptions and maintain essential operations during and after disasters.

- **Improves business resilience:** BCDR ensures that organizations can bounce back quickly after a crisis. It enhances their resilience by enabling them to recover swiftly and continue serving customers, even during challenging times.

- **Enhances data protection:** A robust BCDR strategy safeguards critical data. Whether it's customer information, financial records, or intellectual property, having backup systems and recovery processes ensures data integrity and availability.

- **Enhances compliance:** Many security laws, regulations, and standards have specific sections relating to disaster recovery and business continuity. Adhering to these standards not only avoids penalties but also builds trust with stakeholders.
- **Reduces costs:** Without BCDR, organizations can suffer significant financial losses due to prolonged periods of downtime. A well-executed plan minimizes revenue loss, prevents reputational damage, and maintains investor confidence.
- **Supports competitive advantage:** Organisations with effective BCDR plans demonstrate reliability and preparedness. This can set them apart from competitors, attract clients, and enhance their overall market position.

9.4.2 Differences between BCP and DRP

While business continuity and disaster recovery are closely related, they describe two subtly different approaches to crisis management that businesses can take. There are no major differences between the BCP and the DRP in terms of process flow; that is why most organizations are now treating the two elements in combinations. You should, therefore, understand the difference between these two concepts to be in a position to proffer relevant advice and insight when required.

- **Disaster Recovery Plan (DRP):** A DRP is a form of a contingency plan for how an enterprise will recover from an unexpected event. DRPs help businesses manage different disaster scenarios, such as massive outages, natural disasters, and many others.

- **Business Continuity Plan (BCP).** A BCP serves a critical role in disaster recovery and helps organizations return to normal business functions when a disaster happens. A BCP focuses more broadly on various aspects of preparedness.

Table 9.1 specifies the key differences between the BCP and the DRP.

Table 9.1   Difference Between BCP and DRP

Criteria	BCP	DRP
Focus	Pursues a broad approach covering overall business functions Involves all business units and stakeholders	Focuses specifically on IT systems and critical data. Primarily IT-focused, involving IT teams
Objective	Ensures the organization can continue essential operations during and after a disaster.	Protects IT systems and data during an interruption
Scope	Encompasses people, processes, facilities, and technology	Primarily addresses IT infrastructure and data
Approach	Primarily addresses IT infrastructure and data	Primarily addresses IT infrastructure and data
Timeframe	Long-term planning for sustained operations	Short-term response to restore IT services

Criteria	BCP	DRP
Examples of activities involved	Developing alternate work locations, cross-training staff, redundancy, and simulations	Regular backups, failover systems, and data replication

As can be determined from the comparison in Table 9.1, the major difference between the BCP and the DRP is that the BCP takes a proactive approach and seeks to maintain operations throughout the disaster lifecycle, from when a disaster strikes, during the disaster itself, and after. In contrast, the DRP is generally reactive and specifically deals with processes to respond to and recover from a disaster. As a cybersecurity professional, you should ensure that this distinction is clear as it guides the effective development of the BCDR strategy of the organization, with the BCP focusing on critical continuity processes and the DRP focusing on post-disaster recovery processes.

9.5 Cyber Forensics

Cyber forensics refers to all those processes that are undertaken to enable an organization to collect and preserve its IT evidence for legal proceedings. It involves the investigation of various aspects, including data acquisition, analysis, documentation, analysis, and presentation.[50]

9.5.1 Cyber Forensics Procedure

Cyber forensics follows certain predefined steps from the identification of evidence up to its presentation. Figure 9.3 shows the stages involved in cyber forensics.

---

50. Splunk. "What Is Cyber Forensics?" Accessed December 24, 2024. https://www.splunk.com

Figure 9.3 Cyber Forensics Procedure

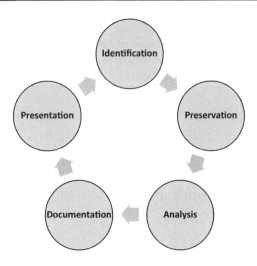

- **Identification:** This is the first step in cyber forensics and involves the identification of the devices and any other resources that might contain data, metadata, or other digital artifacts that might be relevant to the investigation and, therefore, of interest to the cyber forensics investigator. For the best results, you should collect the devices and place them in a forensic laboratory environment or any other security facility that supports data recovery.

- **Preservation:** During the preservation stage, cyber forensic experts create an image or a bit-for-bit copy of the data that is to be preserved. Both the image and the original data should be stored in a secure environment to protect them from alteration or damage. The data can either be persistent (stored on the device's local hard disk drive) or volatile (resident in memory or motion). As volatile data is ephemeral, it should be handled carefully as it can be lost if the device shuts down or power is lost.

- **Analysis:** The analysis stage involves cyber forensics investigators analyzing the captured images to identify relevant digital evidence. This encompasses intentionally or unintentionally deleted files, internet browsing history, and emails, among other digital assets. The major aim is to uncover hidden data or metadata, and this may involve the application of specialized techniques, including live analysis and reverse steganography. With live analysis, you can evaluate still-running systems for volatile data, and with the reverse steganography technique, you can conceal sensitive information within ordinary messages.
- **Documentation:** This is critical in presenting data during legal proceedings. All the stages involved in the data collection process should be described and documented. The judiciary would mainly be interested in whether the data has been tampered with, modified, or otherwise contaminated during its collection and storage processes. This is referred to as the chain of custody. Any tampering with the forensic evidence will likely result in it not being admissible in legal proceedings.
- **Presentation:** Forensic data should offer a structured overview of the extracted insights that can allow a reasonable person to reach a certain conclusion. During the presentation stage, cyber forensic experts will create a formal report outlining their analysis. This report will vary depending on the cases dealt with but should include the forensic investigation findings and any conclusions or recommendations. The reports should then be presented in a court of law as evidence in legal proceedings.

9.5.2 Use of Cyber Forensics

There are several areas in which organizations can apply cyber forensic principles and practices, including the following:

- **Criminal investigations:** Cyber forensics is used by law enforcement agencies and computer forensics investigators to solve computer-related crimes.[51] These crimes often differ depending on jurisdictions and can range from cyberbullying to hacking, software piracy, internet fraud, and identity theft. Cyber forensics can also be extended to provide evidence in physical crimes such as robbery, kidnapping, and murder. For example, law enforcement officials might use computer forensics on a suspect's personal computer to locate potential clues such as deleted files.

- **Civil litigation:** Cyber forensics can also be applied in civil litigation cases such as fraud, employment disputes, or divorces. For example, in a case of Intellectual Property (IP) theft, cyber forensic investigators can recover deleted information from media devices to prove illegal use of copyrighted software. Another example is in a divorce case where a spouse can use mobile cyber forensics to prove a partner's infidelity and apply for a more favorable ruling from the jury.

- **Intellectual Property (IP) protection:** Computer forensics assist law enforcement agencies in investigating intellectual property theft, such as theft of trade secrets. For example, when employees resign or leave their organization, they can sell trade secrets to their former employer's competitors. Cyber forensics allows an organization to identify ex-employees who may have

---

51. "What Is Computer Forensics? | IBM," May 2, 2023. https://www.ibm.com

stolen the information through the analysis of digital evidence.

- **Corporate security:** Organizations can also use cyber forensics following a cyberattack, such as a ransomware attack, to identify the attack vectors and assist in remediating any security vulnerabilities. For example, hackers may leverage a firewall vulnerability to break into your systems and steal sensitive information. Cyber forensics allows you to identify how this would have happened and assists you with valuable information necessary for devising countermeasures.

- **National security:** Computer forensics has also become a crucial tool in the maintenance of national security worldwide. This is due mainly to the increase in cybercrimes among nations, some being undertaken by state actors. Through the use of cyber forensic techniques, governments are able to discover evidence of the origins of cyber-attacks and fortify their defenses.

Chapter Summary

- An incident refers to any event that disrupts operation, including malware infections and social engineering attacks.

- The incident response process consists of four main phases: preparation; detection and analysis; containment, eradication, and recovery; and post-incident activities.

- Containment blocks the lateral movement of an incident through organizational networks, while eradication removes the root cause of the incident.

- During the post-incident activity stage, you often gain valuable lessons that you can use to improve incident handling in the next cycle of the incident response processes.

- BCDR encompasses all the processes that are undertaken to enable an organization to return to normal operations after having experienced a disaster.

- BCDR is one of the most critical elements that should be the focus of cybersecurity professionals, as any failure to resume operations on time may prove catastrophic to the organization.

- The cybersecurity professional should ensure that the assessment of BCDR operations is done regularly, with most standards recommending on a quarterly or annual basis.

- Failing to resume operations on time can be devastating to an organization's operations, hence the need for clear and effective planning.

- The cybersecurity professional should ensure that BCDR operations are subjected to regular tests, with most standards recommending quarterly or annual evaluations.

- Backups of files, equipment, data, and processes are included in BCDR, as are business continuity, business impact analysis, disaster declaration, activities, and programs aimed to restore the firm to an acceptable state RPO and RTO.
- BCDR is critical for risk management, resilience, data protection, regulatory compliance, financial stability, and competitive advantage. It assists enterprises in reducing the impact of disruptions and returning to operations promptly.

Quiz

1. A healthcare organization is planning to undertake an effective incident response process and has set up a team of skilled technical personnel for the purpose. What phase of the NIST incident response lifecycle is the organization currently in?
   a. Detection
   b. Analysis
   c. Containment, eradication, and recovery
   d. Preparation

2. Which phase of the NIST incident response lifecycle is associated with the cybersecurity professional accurately identifying and assessing incidents?
   a. Detection and analysis
   b. Preparation
   c. Containment, eradication, and recovery
   d. Post-incident activity

3. After detecting malware, a cybersecurity analyst proceeded to block network traffic to and from infected IP addresses to prevent the malware from spreading laterally within the organization. Which aspect of the containment, eradication, and recovery phase does the analyst's action represent?
   a. Containment
   b. Eradication
   c. Recovery
   d. Analysis

4. Which of the following actions involves the restoration of data from backups for the purpose of rebuilding damaged systems after a cyber incident?
   a. Resilience
   b. Eradication
   c. Recovery
   d. Business continuity

5. Which of the following actions would you carry out as part of your post-incident activities?
   a. Analyzing root causes
   b. Assigning recovery personnel
   c. Setting recovery budget
   d. Quarantining infected systems

6. An organization seeks to improve its incident response by ensuring that all its employees are aware of their responsibilities and the tools available for use in containing and responding to cyber incidents. Which of the following does this approach represent?
   a. Monitoring response actions
   b. Investing in security training
   c. Establishing effective communication
   d. Reporting to security incidents

7. Which of the following processes should be in place to ensure that incident response teams can swiftly respond to cyber incidents?
   a. Adequate security budget
   b. Certified incident responders
   c. Monitor response actions
   d. Effective communication

8. Why would you advise your organization to regularly test its incident response plan?
   a. To keep the information up to date.
   b. To distribute the plan to stakeholders
   c. To facilitate training
   d. To assess plan implementation

9. Which of the following should an organization focus on if it seeks to resume normal operations quickly after a disaster to prevent catastrophic consequences?
   a. Security alerts
   b. Business Continuity and Disaster Recovery (BC/DR)
   c. Post-incident activity
   d. Proper incident handling

10. Why would you advise an organization to divide its BCDR activities into business continuity and disaster recovery?
    a. To reduce costs
    b. To focus on containment and eradication
    c. To address different aspects of returning to normal operations
    d. To reduce the need for security training

Answers

1 – d	2 – a	3 – a	4 – c	5 – a
6 – b	7 – d	8 – d	9 – b	10 – c

CHAPTER 10
Cloud Security

Key Learning Objectives
- The benefits of migrating to the cloud
- The various cloud service models and cloud deployment models
- Evaluating the cloud security controls

One of the key emerging areas that cybersecurity professionals should be conversant with is how to secure data in the cloud. As most organizations are migrating to the cloud, cybersecurity professionals should be able to implement, manage, and evaluate the security controls in existence, including their adequacy and effectiveness in mitigating cloud security risks. This chapter will introduce you to the concept of the cloud and the steps and actions you need to take to ensure the security of the cloud.

10.1 Introduction to Cloud Security

Cybersecurity professionals are crucial in protecting cloud environments and securing the confidentiality, integrity, and availability of cloud data. Cloud computing is the virtual processing of organizational data. This means that there is no need to purchase any hardware as the data is stored in a virtual version and delivered over the internet. It is as if you have a server and you divide it into multiple servers that are not visible to the user. All the virtual servers will work independently but will share the same physical server. The mechanisms of cloud computing consist of the following characteristics:

- **On-demand self-service:** With on-demand service, you can unilaterally provision your cloud computing capabilities without any assistance or human intervention. For example, you can configure your files and pictures to automatically back up in your Dropbox or iCloud without human interaction in the form of a Cloud Service Provider (CSP)

- **Broad network access:** This is the capability provided by the internet and should be readily available for cloud technologies to work. The cloud cannot function without being connected to the internet, and broad network access should promote the use of a wide variety of access platforms, including mobile phones, tablets, or laptops.

- **Resource pooling:** In a cloud all resources are pooled from various sources to serve a variety of customers without them knowing they would be using the same resources. All the customers will be tenants and resources are provided according to their specific requirements,

regardless of their location. Cloud resources include the following:
- Storage
- Processing
- Memory
- Network bandwidth

- **Rapid elasticity:** Rapid elasticity refers to the capability to elastically and typically automatically scale resource provision in line with customer requirements. The cloud customer views these capabilities unlimitedly ready for use at any given time.
- **Measured service.** Cloud systems can optimize themselves automatically through a metering capability in line with requirements. You can specify the volume of resources you need at a given point in time and that is what is precisely going to be provisioned by the CSP; the system is transparent and devoid of any hidden costs.

10.2 Cloud Service Models

These models specify how cloud computing services are delivered to users and comprise the three major types, namely:

- Software as a Service (SaaS)
- Platform as a Service (PaaS)
- Infrastructure as a Service (IaaS)

The above cloud service models are depicted in Figure 10.1, followed by brief explanations:

Figure 10.1   Cloud Service Models

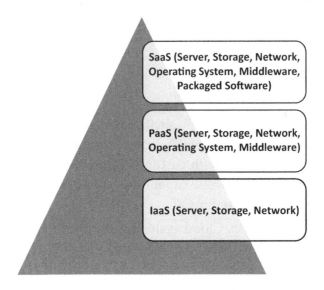

- **SaaS:** A SaaS is a form of cloud service that allows you to deploy applications over the Internet. It reduces the costs associated with the local installation and maintenance of cloud infrastructure and application development platforms.[52] For example, you can access software, such as Microsoft Office 3565, directly from your web browsers without downloads or installations.

- **PaaS:** In a PaaS, you are in between an IaaS and a SaaS, providing you with a platform for building, deploying, and managing your applications. Developers can concentrate on developing high-quality software without worrying about the infrastructure management part of the cloud, thus providing an opportunity to enhance productivity as well. Examples include Google App Engine.

---

52. Lumenalta. "Understanding IaaS vs PaaS vs SaaS vs CaaS | Key Cloud Service Models Explained," December 8, 2024. https://lumenalta.com

- **IaaS:** The IaaS provides the infrastructure required in the cloud and rarely no more beyond that. In an IaaS deployment architecture, you can provision infrastructure such as virtual machines (VMs), storage, and networking resources. Examples of IaaS include Amazon Web Services (AWS) and Google Compute.

Table 10.1 shows the major differences between SaaS, PaaS, and IaaS.

Table 10.1 IaaS vs PaaS vs IaaS

Aspect	SaaS	PaaS	IaaS
Description	Delivers applications over the Internet, eliminating the need for local installation and maintenance.	Provides a platform for application deployment and management.	CSP provides infrastructure in the form of virtual machines, storage, and networking resources
Architecture	Users access software directly from their web browsers without downloads or installations.	PaaS sits between IaaS and SaaS, allowing developers to focus on building and deploying applications without managing the underlying infrastructure.	IaaS offers basic building blocks for cloud infrastructure in terms of networks, storage, and related infrastructure.

Aspect	SaaS	PaaS	IaaS
Management responsibility	CSP is responsible for all management activities.	CSP manages infrastructure, with the customer managing the applications.	CSP manages infrastructure while customer managers platform, operating systems, and software.
Advantages	It is simple as the customer does not manage infrastructure	Simplifies development processes and can be scaled easily	Offers enhanced flexibility as customers onboard preferred add-ons.
Disadvantages	Limited customization opportunities	The customer has less control over infrastructure management	More complex, requiring highly skilled personnel
Examples	Salesforce, Microsoft Office 365	Google App Engine, Microsoft Azure App Service	Amazon Web Services (AWS), Microsoft Azure

10.3 Cloud Deployment Models

Cloud deployment models describe how cloud services are deployed and where they reside. There are three main types:

- **Public cloud:** The public cloud allows anyone to access systems and services. While it provides faster and comprehensive access, its openness makes it less secure. Public cloud infrastructure is owned by the entity delivering the cloud services, not by the consumer. An example is the Google App Engine.

- **Private cloud:** A private cloud is dedicated to a single organization, thus providing the customer with greater control and security. The organization owns and operates its infrastructure, which reduces the incidences of third-party risks.
- **Hybrid cloud:** A hybrid cloud combines both public and private clouds, allowing for data sharing between applications. This allows an organization to leverage the benefits of both models while maintaining flexibility. The hybrid deployment model is useful in organizations in which certain workloads need to remain on-premises while others can be in the public cloud.
- **Community cloud:** In a community cloud, resources are shared by a group of organizations with common interests, such as universities and research institutions. The model allows members to collaborate to define and manage the cloud infrastructure. The results are reduced operating costs due to cost-sharing benefits.
- **Multi-cloud:** The multi-cloud approach involves the use of multiple cloud providers simultaneously, for example, using Google Cloud and Microsoft Azure at the same time. This arrangement allows you to distribute workloads across different clouds to avoid vendor lock-in.

10.4 Importance of Cybersecurity in the Cloud

The following are ways in which effective cybersecurity can improve the security of cloud environments:
- **Improves access control:** Cloud security helps you to ensure that access control is managed responsibly. For example, ensuring that access is revoked to cloud resources when employees leave, and that new

employees are only provisioned with the minimum privileges.

- **Secures access to the cloud:** Integrating cybersecurity principles in the cloud can help you ensure that access to the cloud is secure by verifying that cloud users securely access the organization's cloud. For instance, you can place a requirement that users access cloud resources through an encrypted channel.

- **Enhances the security of APIs and third-party tools:** Because most cloud environments deploy various APIs and third-party technologies, it is crucial to enhance the efficiency and effectiveness of work processes, as these technologies can pose significant security risks. Cloud security assists the organization to identify vulnerabilities in these systems and devise ways to remediate them.

- **Verifies backup strategies:** Cloud security simplifies the performance of data backups, making them effective and configured properly. SoundCloud's security practices will also ensure that effective and adequate security measures are in place to protect the backups.

10.5 The Shared Responsibility Model (SRM)

The Shared Responsibility Model (SRM) is based on the idea that two or more parties play a dual role in the security of the cloud. This means that security is not the sole responsibility of either the cloud customer or the CSP. Each party has a role to play in enhancing cloud security, depending on the cloud service model adopted and any other factors, including agreements in place. For example, the CSP can install patches on the hardware servers, while the customer is responsible for applying encryption processes to protect cloud data.

10.5.1 Sharing of Responsibilities

The responsibilities shared will depend on the provisions of the Service Level Agreements (SLAs) in place, but the general division of responsibilities is shown in Figure 10.2 below:

Figure 10.2 The SRM

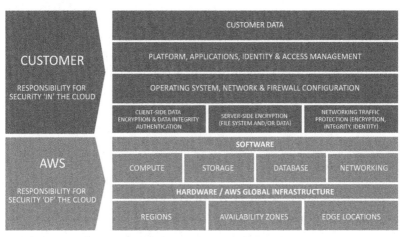

Source: https://aws.amazon.com

As depicted in Figure 10.2 above, customers are typically responsible for security issues involved on user endpoints such as Identity and Access Management (IAM), end-user security and credentials, and the security of workloads and containers. On the other hand, the CSP takes care of the infrastructure management aspects, such as the virtualization layer and network controls. Also, bear in mind that some responsibilities may vary depending on the CSP or the terms outlined in the SLA, for example:

- **Firewall management:** The CSP can assume responsibility for managing the firewall, including the management of configuration, rules, monitoring, and response. While both parties play a role in the security element, the responsibilities are still clearly defined and divided.

- **Cloud data storage:** The CSP can be responsible for all aspects of that cloud data center, including security, monitoring, and maintenance, with the customer retaining responsibility for securing any data within the cloud environment as well as controlling access.

- **Asset protection:** Each party is responsible for the protection of its assets. This means that neither the CSP nor the customer can dictate how or when each party CSP performs its asset monitoring and testing processes.[53] However, the SLA can specify the steps either party should take to ensure the protection and sharing of relevant documentation.

10.5.2 Advantages of the SRM

While a shared security model is complex and requires careful consideration and coordination between the CSP and the customer, the approach offers several important benefits to users. These include:

- **Efficiency:** The SRM enhances efficiency for both the CSP and the customer as they bear respective levels of responsibility. This is akin to the division of labor in the business environment, which allows organizations to concentrate on their core business.

- **Enhanced protection:** CSP would become more focused on the security of their cloud environment and dedicate significant resources to ensuring their customers are fully protected. This may also mean CSPs conducting

---

53. CrowdStrike.com. "What Is the Shared Responsibility Model? | CrowdStrike." Accessed December 24, 2024. https://www.crowdstrike.com

extensive monitoring of customers' security processes and controls. The CSP may also perform timely patching and updating to maintain the required security levels.
- **Improved expertise:** Because CSPs often have a higher level of knowledge and expertise in the emerging field of cloud security due to economies of scale for research purposes, they may be willing to impart this knowledge to their customers. This will assist in enhancing the security of the cloud environment due to the spillover effects of expert customers.

10.5.3 The SRM Best Practices

As organizations migrate to the cloud, they navigate complex territories. As a cybersecurity professional, you can advise such organizations to adopt the following best practices during the process of migrating and operating in the cloud:

- **Carefully review the SLA:** A thorough review of each SLA is critical as security responsibilities differ depending on certain circumstances, such as the type of cloud model, the interest of the CSP, and legal requirements. The cloud environment is also dynamic; you should, therefore, review and reevaluate your contracts to determine if changes or enhancements are required.
- **Prioritize data security.** While cloud customers are always fully responsible for any data stored in the cloud, they may have less expertise in the secure handling and management of that data. However, most likely, the CSP would not be interested in assisting in this regard. You should, therefore, ensure that you develop a robust data security strategy specifically designed to protect cloud-based data.

- **Ensure robust IAM:** Unauthorized access is a grave risk in the cloud environment that can have serious consequences for an organization. The cloud customer is solely responsible for defining access rights to cloud-based resources as well as granting access to authorized users. Ideally, because of the importance of IAM in the cloud, it is crucial to have policies and procedures defining access rights to ensure accountability.

- **Embrace DevSecOps:** You should also embrace the DevSecOps approach as it integrates security continuously throughout the software and/or application development lifecycle. This will assist you in minimizing security vulnerabilities and improving compliance levels in your organization. It is also less costly when vulnerabilities are addressed during the early stages of the Software Development Life Cycle (SDLC). The DevSecOps approach is discussed in more detail in Section 10.6 of this chapter.

- **Implement cloud-native security:** To enhance cloud security, you can also take advantage of the in-built cloud security mechanisms. These include Cloud Security Posture Management (CSPM) and Cloud Workload Protection Platform (CWPP) mechanisms. CSPM focuses on protecting the overall cloud environment including ensuring secure configurations and enforcing security policies. CWPP, on the other hand, focuses on protecting individual workloads such as virtual machines and containers.

- **Identify a trusted cybersecurity partner:** Cloud security is fundamentally different from securing on-premises networks and is dominated by new developments that are constantly evolving. You, therefore, need skilled cloud security professionals to develop and implement cybersecurity strategies and solutions tailored for the cloud. The onboarding of qualified professionals helps in expertly managing all aspects of cloud security from migration to deployment.

10.6 Application Security

Application security refers to all those measures that you implement to protect your application from vulnerabilities and threats. These measures include hardware, software, and operating procedures[54]. For instance, you can deploy a router to prevent individuals from viewing your IP address from the Internet, or you can use an application firewall to strictly define allowed and prohibited traffic into and out of your organizational networks.

10.6.1 Importance of Application Security

Application security is very crucial in the overall security architecture and should form part of the overall security package at any time. Some of the reasons why application security is important include the following:

- **Connection to the cloud:** Modern applications are often available over various networks and connected to the cloud, thus increasing their vulnerability to security threats and breaches.

- **Comprehensive security:** For cloud security to be comprehensive, you should ensure security not only at the infrastructure and network level but also within the applications themselves.

---

54. Biswas, Pretesh. "ISO 27001:2022 A 8.26 Application Security Requirements." PRETESH BISWAS, January 26, 2023. https://preteshbiswas.com

- **Shared resources:** The cloud is a conglomeration of shared resources, and hence it should be handled with care to ensure that users only have authorized access to organizational data. The key takeaway from cloud applications is that they are more vulnerable than on-premise applications as they interface with the public internet.
- **Rise in sophisticated attacks:** Attackers are targeting applications more today than in the past. With the implementation of effective and resilient measures, you can reveal cloud security weaknesses at the application level, helping to prevent these attacks.

10.6.2 Application Security Best Practices

Application security in the cloud poses some extra challenges, hence the need for strict adherence to the best practices that can be adopted. The following is a brief description of some of these practices:

- **Evaluate the CSP's security posture:** The first step in application security is to evaluate the CSP's security posture to identify if there are any gaps and how resilient the environment is. As CSPs do not readily provide customers access to their infrastructure, you may rely on the audit of the CSP in the form of Systems Organisation and Control (SOC) reports. This report provides assessments of the CSP providers' effectiveness of its procedures and policies. They are divided into the following:
  - **SOC 1 Reports:** These reports focus on the financial controls in an organization in terms of their adequacy and operating effectiveness. They are less useful in cybersecurity than SOC 2 reports but are

of greater importance to investors who would like to understand the financial performance of an entity operating in the cloud.

- **SOC 2 Reports:** SOC 2 reports are more extensive than SOC 1 on the five (5) Trust Services Criteria (TSCs), namely: security, data processing, privacy, availability, processing integrity, and confidentiality.[55] They, therefore, are more useful in cybersecurity than SOC 1 reports and come in two forms, that is Type 1 and Type 2. Type 1 reports are produced on a given date and pertain to the assessment at a specific date, while Type 2 covers a period. When assessing the security of the cloud environment, SOC 2 Type 2 is, therefore, the most reliable form of report.

- **Assess the cloud attack surface:** Compared with traditional environments, cloud environments are typically more complex and have less visibility. Most of the assets may also be associated with shadow IT. The cybersecurity professional should use cloud monitoring and observability solutions to determine the cloud's attack surface. The attack surface may consist of cloud instances, containers, and VMs.

- **Adopt a risk-based approach:** You should determine the cloud assets that are at high risk of attack. These should be prioritized and audited first so that remediation steps can be applied before much damage is done to the cloud environment.

  - **Implement encryption:** Encryption is an effective control that can be used to protect applications and sensitive application data from access by cybercriminals. When sensitive data travels with and across

---

55. "The 5 SOC 2 Trust Services Criteria Explained - BARR Advisory." Accessed December 25, 2024. https://www.barradvisory.com

cloud-based applications, it should be encrypted to prevent it from unauthorized access and tampering.

- **Implement logging and monitoring:** If there is a security breach in an application, logging can help identify who got access to the data and how. Application log files should provide a clear record of various aspects regarding the application, who accessed the application, and the time the application was accessed. All this information is critical and assists you in detecting any unauthorized access to the application.

- **Assess the strength of access controls:** As cloud access breaches represent one of the most prevalent cloud security risks, you need to assess the cloud access provisioning process to determine whether appropriate security controls are in place and being complied with. The following are some of the critical areas you may focus on:

    - Presence of strong password standards and policies
    - Implementation of MFA
    - Implementation of the POLP to limit administrative privileges
    - Implementation of ZTA

- **Assess data sharing:** It is also important to ensure the secure implementation of data standards and control data sharing in the cloud. This is because of the data the cloud environment contains, such as personally identifiable information (PII), financial information, and protected medical information (PHI), which is regulated, and the sharing of which should not be permitted. You should also ensure that data loss prevention solutions are in place and that their configuration and operating effectiveness are adequate.

10.7 DevSecOps

DevSecOps is an acronym for development, security, and operations that encompasses cultural transformation, automation, and platform design to integrate the security development and operations activities in an organisation. Figure 10.3 depicts the DevSecOps approach.

Figure 10.3   DevSecOps

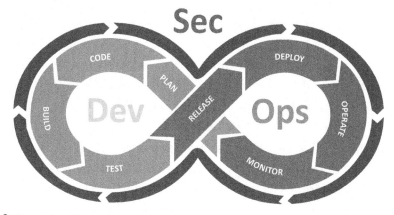

Source: https://www.dynatrace.com

As shown in the diagram above, the development and operations processes are linked in the form of a pipeline from planning to deployment, operation, and monitoring code. The DevOps process starts with planning and then proceeds to coding, building, and testing. These constitute the development phase of the lifecycle. The operations phase consists of release (which comes in the form of a pipeline), deploy, operate, and monitor functions. If we integrate security throughout all these processes, we get what is known as DevSecOps.

10.7.1 Importance of DevSecOps

There are many benefits of adopting the DevSecOps approach in an organization, including the following:

- **Integrates security from the start:** A key benefit of the DevSecOps approach is that it prioritizes security from the earliest stages of planning and development and throughout runtime. This reduces user error at the build and deploy stages and protects while protecting workloads at runtime.

- **Reduces costs:** Because security weaknesses are identified and rectified during the earliest stages, the costs will be low. Generally, costs tend to rise as the stages progress in the SDLC. For example, it is less costly to address a vulnerability during the build stage than to rectify it during the deployment stage.

- **Treats cybersecurity professionals as partners:** Another benefit of the DevSecOps approach is that it treats cybersecurity professionals as partners from the start of DevOps initiatives. This involvement will assist in the inclusion of information security requirements throughout the application development process.

- **Supports security automation:** DevSecOps is also important as it supports security automation in the organization, which helps in reducing the costs associated with security administration activities. The approach enables the establishment and implementation of a clear plan for security automation.

- **Supports strong security culture:** The DevSecOps approach represents a cultural shift towards security in the organization as a whole. It underscores the need to help developers code with security in mind, a process that involves security teams sharing visibility, feedback, and insights on known security vulnerabilities, thus enhancing the overall security culture of an organization.

- **Supports effective risk management:** DevSecOps also focuses on identifying risks to the software supply chain, emphasizing the security of open-source software components and dependencies early in the software development lifecycle.

10.7.2 Components of DevSecOps

Any successful DevSecOps process includes the following components:

- **Continuous integration (CI):** With CI, developers commit their code to a central repository multiple times a day. This approach allows code to be automatically integrated and tested seamlessly within the application development process. Because of this, teams will be in a position to identify integration issues and bugs early rather than waiting until development is complete.

- **Continuous delivery (CD):** CD delivery builds upon continuous integration and automates the movement of code from the built environment to a staging environment. The application is automatically tested in the staging environment and properly integrated. This also ensures that APIs are reliable in handling expected traffic volumes. The result is the organization increasing its ability to consistently deliver production-ready code for the benefit of its customers.

- **Continuous security:** Continuous security involves including security at each phase of the SDLC. It represents a key component of the DevSecOps approach and often incorporates threat modeling and security testing processes. These should be carried throughout the entire application development lifecycle, starting with the developers' own operating environments.[56] Frequently and thoroughly testing software allows for the detection of security issues earlier, which enables the organization to deliver working and secure applications efficiently.

- **Communication and collaboration:** The DevSecOps approach is more successful if there is extensive communication and collaboration within the organization. This is because its functioning is highly dependent on individuals and teams working closely together in delivering secure software. This collaboration is crucial in addressing conflicts in the development process and unifying team members toward common goals.

10.7.3 DevSecOps Best Practices

While organizations can use different approaches in implementing DevSecOps depending on the prevailing circumstances, the following practices will assist you in developing and implementing an effective DevSecOps process:

- **Set clear plans:** Planning is crucial to implementing the DevSecOps approach in the organization. This is because the effects are usually disruptive and, therefore, will require a sense of order from the onset. Start by establishing clear requirements guided by industry and regulatory standards such as OWASP™ Top 10. You can then determine the metric to use in monitoring progress.

---

56. "What Is DevSecOps? Definition and Best Practices | Microsoft Security." Accessed December 24, 2024. https://www.microsoft.com

- **Shift the culture:** There is a need to recognize that adopting DevSecOps involves people who may have a difficult time changing the way they work. This may lead to conflict during the changeover process. It is, therefore, necessary to change their culture through education and effective communication. This will allow them to clearly understand the benefits of the shift and how they fit in, enhancing their acceptance of the new security culture.

- **Standardize your environment:** It is also necessary to ensure that the IT environment is standardized to allow for the smooth adoption of DevSecOps. Security practices such as Zero Trust and the POLP should also be standardized to allow consistent methods of access to all stakeholders.

- **Automate your environment:** DevSecOps works better in an automated environment, and you should ensure you adopt automation to as much an extent as possible. The automation should encompass the automated running of security static analysis tools as part of builds, pre-built container images, and input validation tests, as well as verification authentication and authorization features. Automating the environment allows for the elimination of manual errors.

- **Enhance container security:** General container security is also crucial to the DevSecOps environment. This is achieved through various methods, such as isolating containers and running microservices from each other and the network. It is also important to encrypt data both at rest and traversing between the applications and services to enhance the security of the environment.

Chapter Summary

- Cloud security is crucial for organizations migrating to the cloud, as it helps protect their environments and ensure the confidentiality, integrity, and availability of cloud data.
- Cybersecurity professionals should evaluate existing security controls and their implementation, adequacy, and effectiveness in mitigating cloud security risks.
- Cloud security features include on-demand self-service, broad network access, resource pooling, rapid elasticity, and measured service.
- Cloud security assessments are tests of a cloud environment conducted by an independent third party, ensuring transparency and accountability for both the provider and consumer.
- Cloud security assessments allow an organization to improve its cloud security by providing oversight over access to the cloud and assessing the security of APIs and third-party tools.
- Applications represent a significant attack channel in a cloud environment, and therefore, an organization must enhance the security of its applications to improve the overall cloud security posture.
- An entity seeking to have an appreciation of the CSP's cloud security controls can place reliance on SOC 2 reports as they are more comprehensive and relevant than SOC 1 reports.
- The successful adoption of DevSecOps in an organization depends on various factors including the change in cultural mindset and greater thrust towards automation.

Quiz

1. A cloud customer seeking to provision their computing capabilities without human interaction has approached you for advice as a cybersecurity expert. Which of the following characteristics of cloud computing is the customer looking for?
   a. Broad network access
   b. Resource pooling
   c. On-demand self-service
   d. Measured service

2. Which of the following is a characteristic of computing that allows you to access cloud resources through your mobile phone?
   a. Rapid elasticity
   b. Broad network access
   c. On-demand service
   d. Measured service

3. Which cloud computing characteristic allows the CSP to dynamically allocate resources based on customer requirements?
   a. Broad network access
   b. On-demand self-service
   c. Measured service
   d. Resource pooling

4. Your organization would like to automatically scale its cloud resources in response to fluctuating demands. What is this capability referred to as?

   a. Rapid elasticity
   b. Rapid scalability
   c. Intense flexibility
   d. Measured service

5. You inform your CSP that you intend to pay only for the exact amount of cloud resources you are going to use. Which characteristic of cloud computing are we planning to benefit from?

   a. Broad network access
   b. Exact fee flexibility
   c. Measured service
   d. Resource pooling

6. Which of the following cloud service models allows you to deploy applications over the internet without managing any underlying cloud infrastructure?

   a. Software as a Service (SaaS)
   b. Platform as a Service (PaaS)
   c. Infrastructure as a Service (IaaS)
   d. Storage as a Service (StaaS)

7. Developers in your organization would like to provision a cloud service that allows them a platform to build, deploy, and manage their applications without managing the underlying infrastructure. Which of the service models would advise the organization to provision to meet developer requirements?
   a. Software as a Service (SaaS)
   b. Platform as a Service (PaaS)
   c. Infrastructure as a Service (IaaS)
   d. Identity as a Service (IDaaS)

8. Which of the following cloud services should an organization adopt if it seeks to provision virtual machines, storage, and networking resources in the cloud?
   a. Software as a Service (SaaS)
   b. Platform as a Service (PaaS)
   c. Infrastructure as a Service (IaaS)
   d. Virtualization

9. An organization seeking to leverage both public and private clouds for different workloads and ensure data sharing should adopt which of the following cloud deployment models?
   a. Public cloud
   b. Private cloud
   c. Hybrid cloud
   d. Community cloud

10. You are the cybersecurity analyst at a university that is planning to want to collaborate and share cloud resources with other universities for research purposes. Which of the following cloud deployment models would you advise the universities to adopt?

   a. Public cloud
   b. Hybrid cloud
   c. Community cloud
   d. Multicloud

Answers

1 – c	2 – b	3 – d	4 – a	5 – c
6 – a	7 – b	8 – c	9 – c	10 – c

Glossary

Application security: This refers to all those measures that you implement to protect your application from vulnerabilities and threats.

Application Programming Interface (API): A set of routines, protocols, and tools that are used as building blocks in application development.

Application security: The security aspects that should be observed for an application.

Attack vector: A path or route that is used by the attacker to gain access to the target.

Backup: Resources such as files, equipment, data, and procedures that can be availed for use in the event of an incident or disaster.

Business Continuity (BC): A term that is used to describe all the processes involved in the prevention, mitigation, and resumption of operations following a disaster.

Business Continuity Plan (BCP): A plan that is developed and implemented to guide an organization in responding to the disruption of critical business processes.

Business Impact Analysis (BIA): The process of evaluating the criticality and sensitivity of information assets by determining the impact of losing the support of any resource during a disaster.

Cyber-attack: An actual occurrence of an adverse information security event in an organization.

Cybercrime: A category of crime that involves information technology.

Cyber incident: Actions taken through the use of an information system or network that result in an actual or potentially adverse effect on an information system (NIST).

Cyber forensics (aka digital forensics): A field of forensic science concerned with retrieving, storing, and analyzing electronic data that can be useful in criminal investigations (NIST).

Cybersecurity: A discipline of IT that involves the preservation of the confidentiality, integrity, and availability of information assets.

Cybersecurity controls: Controls relating to an organization's environment in which computer-based application systems are developed, maintained, and operated.

Cybersecurity governance: Leadership, organizational structures, and processes that ensure that the enterprise's cybersecurity programs sustain and extend its strategies and objectives

Cybersecurity governance framework: A model that integrates a set of guidelines, policies, and methods that represent the organizational approach to cybersecurity governance.

Cybersecurity strategy: A long-term plan in which business and IT management cooperatively describe how IT resources will contribute to the enterprise's strategic cybersecurity objectives.

Cloud Computing: a model for enabling ubiquitous, convenient, on-demand network access to a shared pool of configurable computing resources (e.g., networks, servers, storage, applications, and services) that can be rapidly provisioned and released with minimal management effort or service provider interaction. (NIST)

Cloud customer: A person or organization that maintains a business relationship with, and uses services availed by a Cloud Service Provider (CSP).

Cloud Service Provider (CSP): An entity that provides cloud services to interested parties for a fee.

DevSecOps: A cybersecurity paradigm that integrates security in the entire phases of application development and operations.

Disaster: An emergency event that is of such a great magnitude that it overwhelms the organization's capacity to respond. It is typically a considerable time from which to recover.

Disaster Recovery (DR): All the activities and programs that are designed to return an organization to normal operations following a disaster.

Disaster Recovery Plan (DRP): A roadmap that provides a set of human, physical, technical, and procedural resources designed to assist an organization in recovering from a disaster within a defined time.

Database security: All those processes and activities implemented to ensure a database is protected from exposure to attacks.

Data leakage: Any unauthorized transmission of data from an organization to external destinations.

Data Loss Prevention (DLP): Processes, tools, and technologies deployed for preventing data leaks and exfiltration.

Dynamic testing: A form of testing that evaluates software during runtime.

Encryption: The process of applying an encryption algorithm to plaintext that is understandable to a ciphertext that is not easily understandable.

Hashing: A process used in cybersecurity that applies mathematics to generate a fixed-size output from an input of variable size

Identity governance: A set of processes and activities that are used to manage identities within an organization.

Penetration testing: A simulated attack performed by cybersecurity specialists to determine the extent to which attackers can exploit systems.

Public Key Infrastructure (PKI): a framework that provides a set of technologies and processes that are used to protect and authenticate digital communications.

Privileged Identity Management (PIM): Processes that are used to manage access to privileged accounts in an organization.

Recovery Time Objective (RTO): The amount of time it takes for an organization to restore a critical business process after a disaster.

Shared Responsibility Model (SRM): A framework that demarcates responsibilities between the CSP and customer within the cloud environment.

Static testing: A method of software testing that seeks to find errors without running the code.

Virtual Machine (VM): An emulation of a computing environment or operating system that is separate from the host computing system

Virtualization: Adding a guest application and/or data onto an organization's virtual server.

Vulnerability assessment: A process undertaken to systematically identify any weaknesses within organizational systems.

Further Reading

Chimwanda, Elastos. "Essentials for an Effective Cybersecurity Audit." ISACA, April 8, 2022. https://www.isaca.org/resources/news-and-trends/industry-news/2022/essentials-for-an-effective-cybersecurity-audit.

NOTES